Financial Freedom

A Practical Guide to Enhance Earning

(Simple Strategies to Save Invest and Achieve Your Dream)

Timothy Grooms

Published By **Tyson Maxwell**

Timothy Grooms

All Rights Reserved

Financial Freedom: A Practical Guide to Enhance Earning (Simple Strategies to Save Invest and Achieve Your Dream)

ISBN 978-1-7774561-3-9

No part of this guidebook shall be reproduced in any form without permission in writing from the publisher except in the case of brief quotations embodied in critical articles or reviews.

Legal & Disclaimer

The information contained in this book is not designed to replace or take the place of any form of medicine or professional medical advice. The information in this book has been provided for educational & entertainment purposes only.

The information contained in this book has been compiled from sources deemed reliable, and it is accurate to the best of the Author's knowledge; however, the Author cannot guarantee its accuracy and validity and cannot be held liable for any errors or omissions. Changes are periodically made to this book. You must consult your doctor or get professional medical advice before using any of the suggested remedies, techniques, or information in this book.

Table Of Contents

Chapter 1: The Fire Movement

Financial independence and early retirement are two concepts which have captured the attention of people and inspired thousands of people who are looking for a different pathway to a more fulfilling future that is full of freedom in their choices, flexibility, as well as a higher confidence in their lives. The FIRE movement which is an acronym for the powerful blend of Financial Independence and Retire Early It has emerged as an inspiring beacon of light and offers a practical solution to achieving these dreams. In this extensive section, we begin deep exploration into the foundations, theories, and motives driving the FIRE movement. It also focuses on explaining the multitude benefits and benefits which await those who take on and adhere to its transformative idea.

The FIRE movement is rooted in the quest for financial freedom as well as the desire to be free of traditional concepts of retirement. The movement has grown recently due to the efforts of prominent writers, bloggers and communities on the internet committed to sharing their stories and ideas. The trend has now become an all-encompassing phenomenon that is attracting members from different backgrounds who share an objective: to be financially independent and retire in a timely manner.

The underlying principles to the FIRE movement are the three fundamental values: saving, frugality and investing. In adhering to these principles the goal is to establish an impressive nest egg that will allow them to live the life they want and not require conventional work. The premise is founded on the idea that by residing below their income, conserving a substantial amount of their earnings and implementing smart investments and making smart investments, people will accumulate enough wealth enough to afford the lifestyle they want and live a longer life than what is considered to be the typical retirement age.

The appeal of financial freedom and early retirement has many facets. Apart from the obvious advantages of being free from the grind and having more free time The FIRE movement gives a feeling of independence, self-determination as well as control over decisions in life. This allows people to pursue the things they love, try possibilities, and place emphasis on things over the material. Being financially independent can reduce stress levels as well as improved wellbeing, more sense of meaning and satisfaction.

Although FIRE has been a popular topic, and the FIRE movement has earned huge acclaim, it has encountered criticism as well as misinformation. Some argue that retirement early is a huge sacrifice and extreme thrift that aren't feasible or suitable for all. The reality is that retirement is not an all-inclusive plan that can be customized by each individual. their path to fit the values they hold, the circumstances in which they live as well as their goals.

In this article we've explored the fundamental concepts behind FIRE. FIRE movement. We've examined its roots concepts, motives, the motivations and the potential advantages. When you begin your path towards financial freedom and an early retirement, it's vital to determine your ability and set goals that are meaningful, as well as understand the emotional and mental factors of the process. The FIRE movement promises of a lifetime of financial independence and self-confidence The chapters to come will provide you with the steps, decisions and mental shifts that are needed to attain this impressive target.

Chapter 2: Assessing Your Current Financial Situation

When you are on the path to the goal of financial freedom and early retirement understanding your current financial position is crucial. This chapter focuses on the significance of taking a look at your financial situation, and guides you through the procedure of collecting data, analysing the income stream, evaluating your expenses as well as calculating the net worth of your assets. When you conduct a thorough analysis, you will discover valuable information about the financial health of your business and create an excellent foundation that will lead you to the financial independence you deserve.

For a complete review, start by collecting the financial information you have. That includes gathering information on your expenses, income as well as assets, liabilities as well as investments. Make use of tools and resources including financial statements bank statements, pay stubs and summaries of investment accounts to guarantee accuracy and completeness. When you organize and track the information effectively it will give you a more understanding of your financial picture.

Armed with finances, look over your streams of income. Examine the potential growth, stability as well as alignment with your goals in the long run for every source of income. Examine the success of your present efforts to earn more money through investments or side hustles. Recognizing opportunities to diversify and increase your income sources could significantly affect your progress toward financial freedom.

After that, carefully examine the way you spend your money and make lifestyle decisions. Do a thorough review of your budget and habits, and then identify the areas in which you could cut or eliminate expenditures. Review your choices in relation to your daily routine and think about the compromises you can make between the immediate pleasure and your long-term financial ambitions. If you adopt a more thoughtful way of your spending habits, you are able to shift funds to investments and savings.

Find your net worth that is a gauge of your financial stability. Review your assets, such as investment, cash as well as real estate and any other items of value. Add your obligations including student loans, mortgages, credit card debt, as well as personal loans. The calculation gives a clear picture of your financial standing and can help you identify areas of improvements.

Debt assessment is a essential aspect of the financial evaluation. Explore different forms of debts, and consider charges, repayment conditions and their overall effect on your financial objectives. Create strategies for managing and manage debt more effectively and in accordance with your objectives and helping you achieve financial freedom.

Alongside debt check your savings and emergencies money. Examine your savings rates and make sure it is in line with the timeframe you want to achieve financial freedom. Examine the effectiveness of your emergency savings account that is a vital protection in case of emergencies. In optimizing your savings, and establishing a strong financial cushion, you increase the security of your finances.

Then, you should analyze the results of your investment portfolio. Analyze the risk, returns and diversification of your portfolios which include bonds, stocks and mutual funds as well as real property. Examine key benchmarks and metrics to evaluate the efficacy of your investment plan. Change the balance of your portfolio whenever needed to keep it in line with your financial objectives.

When you conduct a thorough analysis of your financial position You can gain insight into the strengths and weaknesses of your financial situation. Knowing where you are in terms of financial standing is the basis for setting significant goals and objectives. In the following chapter we'll explore how to set objectives for your finances and creating the roadmap toward financial freedom and an early retirement.

Chapter 3: Building A Strong Foundation Budgeting And Saving

To achieve the goal of financial independence and earlier retirement, budgeting and savings are fundamentals to a sound financial base. This chapter focuses on the significance of budgeting and savings by guiding you through the steps of making a budget, keeping track of the amount of money you earn and spend, using clever strategies for saving, as well as overcoming the common obstacles. When you master these essential techniques, you can are able to set the foundation for reaching your financial goals as well as achieving your dream of financial freedom.

Budgeting is an essential tool that allows you to get control of your financial situation. It acts as a plan to manage your earnings as well as expenses, and allows you to manage your money wisely. Through the process of creating a budget you will have a better picture of your finances' flow and outflows. This allows you to make informed choices regarding how best to use your funds.

For a start, evaluate your earnings and expenditures. Find out your different sources of income such as regular income as well as side hustles and the occasional cash-flows. Sort your expenses into categories, keeping track of all fixed costs such as mortgage and rent, as well as variables like grocery bills or transportation as well as entertainment. This thorough analysis will provide an overall perspective of your financial position.

If you have a good grasp of the financial environment With a clear understanding of your financial situation, it's time to develop a sensible budget. Take note of your expenses and income to ensure the budget you create is in line with your financial goals as well as goals. Create goals for various areas of spending, while taking into consideration your budgetary obligations, your lifestyle as well as savings goals. Make sure that your budget is able to strike a good balance between satisfying the immediate requirements and fostering your goals for the future.

The use of budgeting methods will make the process feasible and efficient. Examine different budgeting techniques including an envelope-based system the 50/30/20 rule and zero-based budgeting. You can also use online budgeting applications. Choose a method that is compatible with you, and fits the style of budgeting you prefer. The importance of consistency and discipline is for maintaining a successful budgeting routine.

Alongside budgeting, saving is one of the most important aspects to establishing a solid financial base. Saving helps you build up money for investments, emergencies as well as long-term objectives. Use smart strategies to save that are effective for you, like making yourself the first to pay by assigning a part of your income into savings, automating transfer to designated savings accounts and discovering creative methods to lower expenditures and boost savings.

Saving and budgeting aren't easy tasks. The unexpected expenses, temptations to go overboard, or life changes can cause obstacles on the path. If you are able to anticipate and preparing for these obstacles and preparing for them, you will be able to tackle the issues. Discover strategies to conquer the obstacles in budgeting, including making realistic goals, using discipline, seeking out accountability from your financial advisor or the people in your community, and gaining satisfaction in the gains that you have made.

Be sure to create an emergency fund as a crucial component of your financial security cover. Set aside 3 to 6 months of your living costs in a separate easy-to-access account. The savings can provide an insurance policy in the event of unexpected circumstances, and will help you move towards financial independence.

Monitor and regularly adjust your budget in accordance with changes in your circumstances and goals. Examine your budget every month or every quarter, evaluating the progress you have made and identifying points to improve. This will help you remain on the right track and make the necessary adjustments and keep a balanced budget.

The bottom line is that budgeting and savings are the pillars that financial independence can be created. By implementing a budget that is effective it is possible to gain control of your finances and are able to make decisions that are aligned with your priorities. Saving helps you accumulate assets for your short-term needs as well as long-term ambitions. If you can master these important techniques, you can build an enduring financial base which will allow you to achieve an eventual financial security and an early retirement.

Chapter 4: Debt Management And Elimination

It can become a huge obstruction to financial independence as well as an early retirement. In this article we will discuss methods for efficiently managing and eliminating debt. This will allow you to take control of your financial position. Through understanding the different kinds of debt, creating an effective repayment plan in conjunction with proactive steps that will help you take the necessary steps to achieve debt-freedom.

In the beginning, it's essential to know the many kinds of debts that could burden you. Student loans as well as mortgages, personal loan and auto loans are all common instances. Every type of debt has particular characteristics including the rate of interest, repayment conditions and the possible negative consequences. When you know these aspects will help you assess the effects of your debt on your financial well-being.

Examining the state of your debt is the first step to developing a strategy for your repayment.

Review your current obligations, which includes the amount due in addition to interest rates and the minimum payments per month. Find your debt-to income ratio, that is the proportion of your income that goes to payments for debt. This report provides an accurate view of your present debts and obligations. It also helps prioritize your efforts to repay debt.

If you have a thorough understanding of your debts in the first place, you will be able to develop an effective strategy for repaying debt. The most popular strategies include the debt snowball strategy which involves making smaller payments before you tackle the debt avalanche strategy that focuses on the debts that have the highest rates of interest. Pick a method that works to your needs, preferences as well as your financial circumstances and the motivation of your mind.

Develop a debt repayment strategy with specific goals. This can be accomplished by making a list of your debts' priorities, and then determining monthly payment that you can be able to afford. You can use online tools or spreadsheets to keep track of the progress you make and visualize the steps to reduce debt. Make sure to celebrate milestones as you go along to remain motivated and keep the momentum.

Debating with creditors is a crucial part of debt management. Find ways to reduce the interest rate, alter the terms of repayment, or even pay off your debts. A successful negotiation will significantly lessen the burden on the debt you owe. Debt consolidation can also be an option that can reduce the burden of repayment by consolidating multiple loans into one easier to manage installment. But, be sure to carefully consider the conditions and costs prior to making a decision on this route.

For faster repayment of debt think about strategies for increasing your income via extra jobs, cutting down on expenditures, or shifting resources out of non-essential parts of your budget. Each dollar you put into the repayment of debt will bring the possibility of financial freedom.

When you are working toward eliminating debt it is vital to establish financially sound practices. Saving, budgeting and making sure you are mindful about spending are the key elements of living a debt-free life. When you adopt these practices will help you avoid the accrual of credit and help ensure financial security.

Professional assistance for example, counseling for debt or credit programs, may provide invaluable assistance on the road to debt relief. They offer advice from experts on negotiation, as well as customized strategies to tackle the specific debt issues you have. You should ensure that you select reputable companies that will serve your interests.

The management of your credit score as well as credit history is a crucial element of managing debt. While you are paying off loans, you should concentrate on maintaining and strengthening your creditworthiness. Making timely payments, being responsible with utilization of credit as well as monitoring your credit score are essential to longer-term financial security.

Although the path towards debt-free living may be filled with obstacles, staying focused is essential. Accept that you may face setbacks and you'll have to fight through them. Be grateful for each achievement you have made and be grateful for the accomplishments you've accomplished. By focusing and a disciplined approach you will be able to conquer the burden of debt, and get closer to your financial freedom and earlier retirement plans.

Effective control of debt and its elimination is vital to achieve financial independence. When you understand your debts and devising a repayment plan and implementing proactive steps to stay motivated to take control over your financial situation. Make a decision today to get rid of financial burdens and open the way for an uninvolved and financially secure the future.

Chapter 5: Maximizing Income Career Advancement And Side Hustles

When you are on the road to early retirement and financial independence maximising your earnings plays an important part. Chapter 5 explores methods and options for increasing the amount you earn through professional advancement and side work. If you evaluate your current financial and expenses, putting money into your career development by negotiating the benefits and salary, pursuing opportunities for side hustles and using the internet to find new ways to finance expansion.

For starters, you should take an in-depth look at your income and financial situation. Examine your earnings and bonuses, commissions, or other forms of pay. Think about the future growth possibilities and align your current job or career to your financial objectives for the long term. Being aware of where you stand in terms of financial standing is an excellent beginning point to determine what steps to make to boost your income.

Making the investment in your career's advancement an effective strategy to increase the amount you earn. Learning continuously, continuing professional development as well as acquiring advanced skills will make you eligible for increases in your salary, promotions as well as higher paying opportunities. You may want to consider pursuing higher-education and certifications or seeking for mentorship opportunities that will enhance your abilities and broaden the possibilities of your career.

Negotiating your salary and benefits can be a the best way to boost your earnings. Learn to negotiate effectively as well as research rates in the market to assess your value on the market for jobs. When you negotiate, make clear your achievements, abilities as well as the value that you can bring to your company. Through advocacy in negotiations, you could secure greater pay, better benefits and other types of pay that will help the growth of your finances.

Freelancing and side hustles is an alternative way to increase the amount of money you earn. Side jobs provide extra income streams in addition to your main job. They are a viable option across a variety of industries including online companies or e-commerce. They can also be part of the gig economy or other innovative ventures. Examine your interests, skills as well as your time available to find possibilities for side hustles that are in line with your strengths as well as financial targets.

The ability to balance multiple streams of income requires an effective time managing and prioritizing. Establish clear boundaries and set specific time to your other responsibilities as long as your career remains your top first priority. Make use of productivity strategies and automated devices to simplify your work and increase your productivity. If you can manage your income streams effectively, you'll be able to maximize the potential of your earnings without degrading the overall health of your family.

Make use of online platforms and technologies to increase your earnings potential. Platforms online provide an array of array of options including freelancing platforms such as e-commerce marketplaces or content-creation platforms. They allow the user to show their skills and connect with customers or clients, and earn money. Make use of the potential of technology to increase your reach, and gain access to the world market.

Examine the viability financially of any side hustles you might consider before making a decision to invest. Do thorough research including estimates of revenue, cost analysis as well as market demand assessments. Utilize a data-driven method to assess the viability and viability of every side hustle. When you allocate your time and energy wisely you will be able to ensure that your side hustles add positively to your success in your financial goals.

Making passive streams of income is another way to increase the potential of your earnings. Look into opportunities for investment properties for rental, dividends royalty, online training courses. A passive income can provide a consistent source of income that needs minimal effort to establish once it has been established. When you diversify your sources of income as well as creating income streams that are passive it is possible to create ongoing financial stability, and aid your efforts towards financial freedom.

To conclude, maximising the amount of money you earn through your career as well as side-hustles is a crucial aspect of your road to financial security or early retirement. Through assessing your income and spending money on professional development as well as negotiating efficiently and exploring other opportunities, as well as leveraging platforms on the internet that offer the doors to financial success. Be a part of the process of constantly looking for ways to increase the potential of your earnings, and you'll soon be on the way to reaching your goals in the financial realm.

Chapter 6: Frugal Living And Mindful Spending

Spending wisely and living a frugal lifestyle is a must-have for achieving financial freedom as well as early retirement. In this section we will explore the fundamentals and methods of living frugally that will help you choose wisely with your money. It is also a good idea to place a greater emphasis on long-term financial goals than immediate gratification. Through understanding the advantages of thrift, reviewing your consumption habits, establishing an affordable budget, accepting minimalist living, and engaging in the art of conscious consumption, you'll be able to create a sustainable and satisfying lifestyle financially.

Living a frugal lifestyle is about taking an intentional approach to spending, and making conscious choices about your spending. This requires changing your perspective towards value-driven rather than consumption-oriented. When you prioritize value over cost it is about gaining maximum benefit and enjoyment from each cent you spend. It is a good idea to consider the value of your wants and needs as well as distinguish between necessary or discretionary costs as well as eliminate any the unnecessary or unproductive expenditure.

In order to begin living a frugal lifestyle examine your present budgeting practices. Spend time to take the time to monitor your spending and examine patterns of the spending habits you have. You can identify areas where you are able to adjust your spending and cut back on spending that isn't necessary. When you understand your habits of spending it helps you become aware and gain the ability to control your spending.

Making a budget that is frugal is the first step towards aligning your spending to the goals of your finances and personal values. Make realistic expectations for the various areas of spending, including transport, housing foods, entertainment, and transportation. Find ways to maximize expenditure, including the search for cost-effective alternatives or reducing non-essential expenditures, and pursuing offers or reward programs. A budget with a reasonable amount of money provides guidelines for spending responsibly that allows you to set priorities for the financial goals you want to achieve.

The smart shopping approach and the consumer strategy are essential to budget-friendly living. Shopping for bargains, utilizing coupons and reward and discounts, making purchases prior to purchase could result in substantial savings. When you make deliberate and educated making purchases, you will stay clear of impulse buys and make sure that you spend your money carefully.

Decluttering and embracing minimalism is a prerequisite for thrifty living. The concept of minimalism helps you evaluate the things you own, consider the things that truly enrich your life, and then let the excess material items. The process of decluttering your space will not only help create a more well-organized environment, but it also aids you be aware of the things you add to your daily life. If you adopt a minimalist approach to life it is possible to cut down on expenditures and instead focus on your experiences and satisfaction.

Conscious consumption and mindful spending are essential to spending less. If you're aware of your needs, values and goals for the long term it is possible to make thoughtful decisions with your money. Think about the effects of every decision on the financial objectives and your overall wellbeing. By focusing on conscious consumption, you are able to focus your money on your priorities as well as reducing the amount of waste and expenses that are unnecessary.

When frugal living is focused on cutting costs however, it is crucial to establish an equilibrium between spending less as well as quality of living. This isn't about denying yourself or forgoing enjoyment. It's more the act of making conscious choices which prioritize financial security for the long run but still leaving the space to enjoy moments, health and overall well-being. If you are able to allocate your money sensibly and taking pleasure in the simplest pleasures of life, you will be able to find a way to balance both your financial goals as well as the overall quality of your living.

Being able to overcome challenges and remain motivated to live a frugal life is vital. It's normal to encounter challenges and doubts However, by focusing on your goals for financial success and embracing the accomplishments you achieve it is possible to maintain the motivation. Rejoice in the milestones that you reach and keep in mind the benefits that will come from the habit of frugality that is sustainable.

Conclusion: Frugal lifestyle and conscious spending is a transformative practice that can help your progress towards financial independence as well as early retirement. If you adopt the tenets of frugality reviewing the way you spend money, developing an efficient budget, adopting the concept of minimalism and embracing the art of conscious consumption, you can attain financial freedom and live an intentional and satisfying lifestyle. Be awed by the value of saving money and let it influence your choices in the direction of the most sustainable and brighter tomorrow.

Chapter 7: Investment Basics

Understanding different Asset Classes Investment is one of the most important aspects to getting financial freedom and accumulating wealth. In this chapter, we explore the basic principles of investing through studying various asset classes. Knowing the different asset classes, such as bonds, stocks the real estate market, the cash equivalents and commodities can be crucial to creating an asset portfolio with diversified diversification. If you are aware of the traits as well as the risks and potential returns of every asset class and asset class, you are able to make well-informed investments that are in line with your goals in terms of financials.

In the beginning, it's crucial to understand the importance that investing plays in the process of achieving financial freedom. They can provide an increase in capital value and passive income, and also protection against inflation. Utilizing the strength of various asset types to increase your wealth while achieving your financial independence.

Let's begin by discussing assets classes and the importance they play for portfolios of investment. Asset classes are a grouping of investment with the same traits and behavior. Major asset classes comprise bonds, stocks and real estate as well as commodities and cash equivalents. Each asset type has distinct characteristics and possible returns which allow buyers to expand their portfolios as well as control risk efficiently.

Stocks are the representation of ownership in public companies. The following article explores the basics of the stock market, including the equity of ownership, its potential risk and return. We look at different kinds of stock, including general stocks that provide the option of dividends and voting rights in addition to preferred stocks with fixed dividends and only limited vote rights.

On their own are investments with fixed income. This article explains the idea of bonds issuers and interest rates and coupons. Corporate bonds, government bonds, as well as municipal bonds are just a few of the varieties of bonds one can look at. Bonds provide an ongoing stream of revenue through regular interest payment which makes them appealing for investors who are cautious about risk and want reliable yields.

The real estate market is yet another important asset type. It is an investment possibility that can be tangible by talking about residential and commercial properties, as well as real estate trusts (REITs). Real estate investment offers the possibility of rent income as well as long-term appreciation offering stability and diversification to your portfolio of investment.

Commodities are the investment in natural and physical resources. The commodities we introduce are precious minerals, energy resources agricultural commodities, as well as industrial metals. Commodities can be purchased direct through the use of futures contracts, as well as indirectly through commodities-based shares and exchange-traded fund (ETFs). They provide a protection against inflation and act as a way to diversify an investment portfolio that is well-balanced.

The cash equivalents that are available, which include the money market fund, certificates of deposits (CDs) and Treasury bills provide security and stability as well as liquidity. The purpose of cash equivalents within the investment portfolio, and also the way they function as an safe refuge during volatile market circumstances.

Diversification and allocation of assets are fundamental concepts when establishing the investment portfolio. It is crucial to consider diversifying investments across various types of assets to reduce the risk efficiently. Through diversifying the portfolio you are able to lessen the effect of each investment class's performance on total investment return.

Knowing the relation between return and risk is essential in making investment decisions. The following article will discuss the different risk-based profiles for various categories of asset and guide readers identify their tolerance to risk. The alignment of risk tolerance and your investment goals is crucial to making a portfolio that is suitable for your comfort as well as your financial objectives.

In the final section, we will discuss various options for investment strategies and vehicles that investors may use. Mutual funds and ETFs, exchange traded funds (ETFs) and index funds are diversified investments. We will discuss the most popular investment strategies like buy-and-hold growth investing, value investing, and dollar cost Averaging. We help readers comprehend the different ways to invest.

The bottom line is that understanding the various kinds of asset classes is crucial in establishing a sound portfolio for investment. When you know the features as well as the risks and return of stocks, bonds and real estate, as well as commodities and cash equivalents You can make educated decision-making about your investments. Diversification across asset classes as well as the alignment of your portfolio to your personal risk tolerance as well as investment goals are essential to achieve financial freedom through the investment process. Learn about the various categories of investment as you set off in your journey to invest toward a secure and prosperous financial future.

Chapter 8: Investing For Financial Independence The Fire Approach

The FIRE (Financial Independence Retire Early) trend has seen the momentum of recent years because people are seeking alternative to their traditional working patterns and seek financial freedom. In this article we explore methods and the principles behind making investments to achieve financial independence by with the FIRE method. Through understanding the fundamental aspects of the FIRE model, creating financial goals, establishing solid savings by establishing an investment strategy and maximizing the tax efficiency of your investments, reducing risks, planning for the possibility of early retirement and maintaining an appropriate lifestyle and a balanced lifestyle, you will be paving the way to achieve the financial freedom you desire and an early retirement.

Let's begin by exploring the basic principles that underlie FIRE. FIRE movement. FIRE is a framework for the importance of saving a lot, investing prudently as well as reducing expenditures for financial security. The approach requires a change in perspective to place the focus on long-term financial goals prior to immediate satisfaction. The central element of the FIRE strategy is the idea that there is a "FIRE number" which is the amount necessary to reach financial freedom. Knowing this number gives you the clear direction that you can work towards, and also guides the investment choices you make.

The setting of financial goals as well as determining the most realistic time goals are essential for successful FIRE. Set out clearly your financial goals and think about the life you would like to lead when you retire. Setting a realistic timeline that is based on the amount of money you earn, how much you spend, and investment strategy will assist to keep your focus and motivation throughout the course of your journey.

The creation of a solid savings foundation is the most important aspect of the FIRE strategy. Consider strategies like planning your budget, frugality, and boosting your earnings in order to increase your savings capacity. Setting up an emergency savings account is crucial for you to provide the security of your finances and guard against the possibility of unexpected costs.

Making sure you have a strategy of investing that is in line with the FIRE method is essential to achieve long-term financial freedom. You should consider investing in low-cost diversified index mutual funds, funds and exchange traded funds (ETFs) which are in line with your personal risk tolerance as well as the goals of your investments. A long-term, non-investing approach to investing will allow your investment to increase over time while maximizing the compounding effect of yields.

The ability to maximize tax efficiency could significantly affect your path to financial freedom. Look into tax-advantaged savings accounts, for instance, individual Retirement Accounts (IRAs) as well as 401(k)s in order to limit the burden of tax. Making sure you invest in tax-deductible and tax-advantaged accounts will aid in maximizing your post-tax earnings.

The ability to manage market volatility and risks are essential skills for investors in FIRE. Resilient during fluctuations in the market by keeping a longer-term view and avoid making emotional choices. Apply risk-management strategies such as asset allocation and diversification to safeguard your portfolio from exposure to a single class of asset.

The process of planning for early retirement involves an attentive consideration of the unique issues including health care, Social Security, and withdrawal strategies. Find strategies for earning money when you are in your early retirement years including part-time employment as well as freelance work, or even passive streams of income. You should think about the best way to arrange your retirement and investment strategies so that you can afford your lifestyle through retirement.

Monitor and regularly adjust your FIRE strategy to make sure that it is in line to your objectives. Financial markets and life circumstances are subject to change and require flexibility and ability to adapt. A regular reassessment helps you make the necessary adjustments to stay focused on achieving financial independence.

In order to attain financial independence It is crucial to have the balance of your life. Keep in mind that your goal does not just mean building wealth, but it's also about getting satisfaction beyond the financial gains. Consider your own well-being, friendships and the experiences you have throughout the process.

Getting professional advice for advice, like an investment planner or financial planner knowledgeable of the particular demands that are part of the FIRE movement, could provide important advice and help. They will help you refine your investment strategies, make complicated financial choices, and remain responsible to the goals you set for yourself.

In the end, the FIRE strategy for investing can provide the path to financial security along with early retirement. Understanding the basic principles in this FIRE movement, establishing financial goals, establishing an enduring savings base and establishing an investment plan that maximizes your tax efficiency, managing risks, planning for an early retirement, and ensuring your lifestyle in a healthy way You can be in control of your financial destiny. Take the FIRE method seriously and begin an exciting journey to achieve your financial goals, and enjoy living the life you want to live.

Chapter 9: Tax Optimization And Retirement Accounts

Tax optimization plays an essential function in increasing the accumulation of wealth and reaching longer-term financial goals. In this article we will explore the world of retirement account and discuss ways to optimize your tax situation. Through understanding the different kinds of retirement accounts including traditional IRAs as well as Roth IRAs, 401(k)s, 403(b)s as well as SEP IRAs You can make the most of tax-savings provided by these accounts for increased savings as well as plan for a financially secure retirement.

Optimization of taxes is an essential element of a comprehensive financial plan. Through strategically managing your tax burdens and tax liabilities, you will be able to minimize the tax burden and maximize the returns you earn from your investments. We'll begin by examining the many types of retirement account that are available.

Traditional IRAs permit tax-deductible contributions as well as tax-free growth.

Contributing pretax earnings to reduce your current tax-free earnings while allowing investments to increase tax-free up until retirement. Retirement withdrawals can be taxed as normal income. They can also provide tax benefits if you plan on having an income tax bracket that is lower in your retirement.

Roth IRAs On their own, provide tax-free withdrawals during retirement. Even though making contributions to Roth IRAs is not tax-deductible, their capital growth as well as the qualified withdrawals are tax-free. Roth IRAs are especially beneficial if you plan to fall into an upper tax bracket in retirement.

Retirement plans offered by employers like 401(k)s as well as 403(b)s are excellent vehicles to save for retirement. The contributions to these plans are paid on a tax-free basis, which reduces your tax-deductible income. Certain employers will even match contributions. This can provide an added benefit to your retirement savings. When you withdraw funds during retirement, they are taxable as regular income, deferring tax when you are working can aid in maximizing your tax position.

for self-employed people, SEP IRAs and Solo 401(k)s provide retirement-planning options. These plans permit contributions that are tax-deductible, allowing you to invest in retirement savings while decreasing your tax burden. They have greater contribution limits compared to conventional IRAs which allows for better efficiency in taxation and savings for retirement.

Making the most of retirement savings can be a successful strategy for the optimization of your taxes. If you contribute the highest allowable amount, you will be able to take maximum benefit from tax deductions as well as the possibility of future expansion. You should consider adjusting your budget and financial plan to place retirement benefits within the permitted limitations.

Conversion strategies and rollovers could also help you maximize the savings you can make in retirement. Transferring money from retirement accounts to other retirement accounts, or changing to Traditional in IRAs to Roth could be tax-related. Take note of the tax benefits and tax consequences that could arise from these actions prior to proceeding.

The required minimum distributions (RMDs) are an essential component of the management of your retirement account. Learn the rules and regulations to take RMDs out of retirement accounts so that you don't incur penalties. Develop distribution strategies that work with your tax-related goals, and will help you maximize the duration of the retirement savings you have.

Strategies to invest tax-efficiently further aid in tax efficiency. Asset placement as well as tax loss harvesting as well as managing capital gains, can aid in optimizing after-tax returns and lower tax obligations. Through strategically arranging investments into tax-favored and taxable accounts, you can reduce the impact of taxation on your portfolio of investments.

Tax planning is essential for early retirement. planning. Controlling income sources, limiting taxes, and structuring withdrawals effectively are important factors. Consult a tax professional for help for help in navigating the complex the complexities of early retirement tax plan.

Tax optimization via retirement accounts can be a beneficial way to maximize the accumulation of wealth and having financial security in retirement. Through understanding the various types of retirement accounts, maximising the contributions you make, employing tax-efficient methods, and getting expert tax guidance when needed to optimize your tax position and prepare your self for a successful retirement. Benefits of retirement savings accounts to improve your financial security, and have an enjoyable retirement.

Chapter 10: Building Passive Income Streams

The passive income can be a potent instrument to achieve financial freedom. In this article we look at the concept of passive income, and dive into different strategies to build sources of passive income. Understanding the different kinds of passive income including real estate investments dividend stocks, investments that pay interest royalty, online business and peer–peer lending you are able to create other sources of income which work to your advantage even when you're not involved in the process.

The passive income model has many benefits. It offers financial security through diversifying income streams, and decreasing your dependence on one source of income. In addition, it gives an opportunity for flexibility as well as the possibility of wealth accumulation in time. Let's explore the realm of passive income to discover what possibilities are available.

The investment in real estate is one of the most popular ways for earning passive income. It can be done through rentals and REITs, (REITs) or even rental properties for short-term rentals, real estate investment can provide regular cash flow as well as the potential for long-term appreciation. It is important to know the basic principles of investing in real estate, which includes choices for financing, property selection and the property management aspects.

Dividend investment is a different option for earning passive income. When you invest in dividend-paying stocks, you could earn steady dividends in cash. Dividend investing involves careful stock selection, and an eye on stocks with a track record of regular dividend payouts. The creation of a dividend portfolio may provide an unreliable and increasing source of income that is passive.

Making passive income from bond and interest-paying bonds is an approach that is relatively risk-free. Saver's account, certificates of deposits (CDs) and bonds provide regular interest rates for a period of time. If you choose to invest in instruments with interest that earn you the benefits of passive income and preserve capital. Knowing the tradeoff between risk and return and adopting a diversification strategy is the key to success in this field.

The royalties earned from intellectual property could create the passive income. Making and monetizing intellectual property assets such as music, books trademarks, patents or other intellectual property are able to provide regular income via royalties or licensing agreements. Intellectual property assets could provide an opportunity for steady income, while also leveraging your creativity and knowledge.

Digital and online-based businesses can provide an opportunity to earn passive income. eCommerce, affiliate marketing online classes, as well as digital downloads are only some examples of internet-based businesses that earn the passive income. Establishing an online presence and providing valuable product or content can draw an audience of many and generate reliable revenue streams.

Platforms for crowdfunding and peer-to-peer lending provide alternatives to earning passive income. When you lend funds directly to individuals, or participating in crowdfunding initiatives it is possible to get returns or interest from your stake. It is important to be aware of the potential risks with these platforms as well as do your due diligence prior to taking part.

Growing and securing passive income streams is a process that requires time and a strategic plan. First, you must identify the streams of passive income that match with your preferences, needs and financial objectives. Diversify your income streams from passive sources to lower risk and improve the resilience of your income sources. Continuously evaluate and enhance the passive sources of income so that they are generating long-term returns.

The passive income stream is an essential factor in attaining financial freedom. Through diversifying income sources and creating an income stream that is passive that you can build a strong base for stability in your finances and independence. It is crucial to find the right balance between managing your income streams from passive sources as well as enjoying the benefits from a more flexible and unstructured lifestyle. Find ways to align your passive income activities to your own goals, values, and your ideal lifestyle for satisfaction over the long term.

The conclusion is that creating streams of income that are passive offers the chance to generate different streams of income that are working for you even when you're not active in the business. Through exploring various avenues including real estate investments as well as dividend stocks, investments that pay interest and royalties, internet-based businesses as well as peer-to–peer lending you could earn the passive income you need to meet your financial targets. Make the most of passive income, and set off in the direction of the financial freedom, security and a happier lifestyle.

Chapter 11: Real Estate Investing For Fire

The real estate investment industry has emerged as an effective method for those who are seeking financial freedom and earlier retirement (FIRE). In this section we look into the complexities of real estate investment and how it can be used to the FIRE path. When you are aware of the various ways to invest in real estate by conducting thorough study of the market and analysis of property and analyzing different financing options, taking a look at the possibility of cash flow, implementing due diligence and managing your properties efficiently, you will be able to leverage the benefits of real estate investment to earn an income that is passive and create wealth.

There are many benefits to investing in real estate within the FIRE road. The property can be used to generate money flow, appreciation over the long term and diversification of portfolios. Furthermore, investments in real estate are a tangible asset which can be used to earn passive income as well as provide a consistent cash flow. Let's look into the main elements of investing in real estate to help you achieve FIRE.

Examining strategies to invest in real estate is the initial stage. Look into options for houses hacking, rental properties and REITs, real estate trusts (REITs) as well as crowdfunding for real estate. Each approach has distinct strengths and disadvantages, which is why it's crucial to determine what best suits your needs and goals.

The conduct of thorough market research and property research is essential to discovering potential investment possibilities. Things like location and rental demand, the property's condition and possible returns from investment must be meticulously assessed. Use resources like local market information as well as demographic trends as well as comparable analysis of property for making informed choices.

Understanding the various financing options and mortgage-related considerations is crucial for investors in real estate. Consider traditional mortgages as well as FHA credit, hard cash loans. You should also take into consideration factors such as creditworthiness, the amount of down payment, as well as debt-to-income ratios to secure acceptable conditions for financing. Find the best financing solution that will meet your financial goals and financial needs.

Assessing the potential for cash flow as well as the return of investments (ROI) of the property is one of the most important aspects of investing in real estate. Determine the rental revenue accurately and include costs like maintenance, management of the property, and vacancies. You can estimate ROI to determine that investment properties are profitable. properties. A thorough analysis and precise forecasts of financials are crucial.

Due diligence and acquisition of property is a crucial step to reduce the risk of investing and make wise decision. Perform appraisals, inspections of the property, titles searches and then negotiate acceptable conditions. The diligence you do during this phase can help to identify any potential problems and makes sure that your investment is in a property with high potential for success over the long term.

Achieving effective property management and relationships with tenants are crucial to getting the most value for your money and eliminating stress. Think about self-management, hiring an experienced property manager or using a property management system for smooth operation. Follow best practices for tenant screening leasing agreements, lease collection and maintenance of the property to ensure positive cash flow and ensure satisfaction of tenants.

Knowing the tax benefits in real estate investment is vital to maximize the yields. Benefit from deductions on the mortgage interest, property tax as well as depreciation. Consider strategies such as 1031 exchanges and professional real estate status to maximize the tax advantages and reduce taxes.

The ability to scale and diversify the real estate portfolio is an important consideration for investors who are looking to FIRE. When you gain expertise and knowledge, diversify your portfolio by making investments in various kinds of properties, areas and investment models. Diversification can reduce risks and improves portfolio performance.

Understanding and managing risks in real estate investment is crucial. The fluctuation in the market, vacant properties and unplanned repairs are a few potential risks. Make sure you have enough cash reserves available ensure adequate insurance coverage and make contingency plans to reduce the risk effectively.

The real estate investment can be integrated into your FIRE strategy to speed up the process towards financial independence and an early retirement. Think about how investments in real estate are able to complement other types of assets that you have in your portfolio. Find the right balance, which is in line with your risk tolerance and use real estate into your strategy to earn passive income as well as creating wealth.

To conclude, real estate investing can be a great option for people who want to achieve the goal of financial freedom and early retirement. With a thorough understanding of the different investment strategies, performing an in-depth study and analysis, looking at different financing options, managing the properties efficiently, and minimizing the risks, you are able to utilize real estate investment to create steady income, and build wealth. Make the most of the possibilities offered by investing in real estate in your quest to retire and discover new possibilities that will allow you to live a financially secure and prosperous future.

Chapter 12: Alternative Investments

Side Ventures For those seeking financial freedom as well as early retirement examining alternatives to investing and side ventures could provide fresh opportunities for diversifying your portfolio to earn extra income, and possibly speed up your progress. This chapter will delves into the realm of alternate investment options and side ventures talking about their benefits, risk, and aspects within the FIRE process.

Alternative investments are a great method for diversification of your investment portfolio outside of the traditional investment classes. Commodities and precious metals including gold, silver and agricultural goods could be used as a protection against economic and inflation risks. They provide security and the potential for growth in times of volatility.

The growth of cryptocurrency and digital assets has created numerous investment opportunities. Bitcoin, Ethereum, and decentralized finance (DeFi) provide the opportunity of a significant return, however they also are characterized by high volatility. The investment in cryptocurrency should be handled with care, taking into account the nature of speculation as well as the importance of appropriate managing risk.

Platforms for peer-to-peer lending and crowdfunding provide alternative ways to earn an income that is passive and diversifying your investments. When you lend funds directly to individual investors and participating in crowdfunding campaign and campaigns, you could get returns or interest on the investments. It is important to evaluate the risk return, the risks, and the risk of being unable to liquidate this type of investment.

Making investments in startup companies and venture capital is a great opportunity for risk-free, high-reward investment. In providing capital to young firms or companies that are developing new technologies, you could profit from substantial gains and growth. But, investing in this way needs careful consideration since the chance of failing for startups is very high.

Real Estate Investment Trusts (REITs) provide a way to get exposure to the real estate market. REITs pool investors' funds for investment in a broad portfolio of properties that generate income. They provide the opportunity to profit of real estate properties without directly managing or owning the property.

Entrepreneurship and side projects are also a factor in creating additional revenue as well as diversifying sources of income. Beginning a side-business or making use of your expertise and knowledge can result in new streams of income. The side hustles could be anything from freelance work to consultation to online companies or even passion initiatives. They provide versatility and have the potential for substantial growth.

The investment in collectibles, as well as fine art is a viable asset type that investors can invest in. Coins that are rare, stamps and sports memorabilia fine art could gain value in time. But, investing in these investments requires knowledge, experience as well as an awareness of the risks involved.

Socially Responsible Investment (SRI) and Impact investing provide opportunities to integrate investments into social and personal goals as well as societal impacts. Through investing in businesses and funds that support the environment, social, and governance (ESG) concepts Investors can earn financial profits while donating to causes they are passionate about.

In the event of considering alternatives to investing it is essential to consider the risks involved and perform careful due diligence. Consider investment options, take into account the liquidity of your investments, and get a an understanding of the potential options for exit. Alternative investments typically come with distinct risks and considerations that need careful assessment.

Incorporating other investments as well as side ventures in your FIRE plan could complement conventional investment strategies, and could aid in the process of becoming financially independent. Take into consideration your tolerance to risk, your investment allocation and your longer-term financial goals before incorporating alternatives into your overall plan.

To conclude, exploring alternatives to investment options and side ventures offers opportunities to broaden your investment portfolio and earn more income and possibly help you achieve financial freedom as well as early retirement. When you understand the positives, the risks, and aspects of alternatives to investments as well as side ventures, it is possible to make educated decisions that are in line with your objectives and beliefs. Explore the possibilities of alternate investments and side ventures as you move toward financial security and a happier life.

Chapter 13: Designing Your Ideal Early Retirement Lifestyle

When you're looking to achieve the ideal early retirement age, it is essential to think about not only the financial aspects but the kind of lifestyle you want to live. Chapter 13 is a look at the notion of creating your ideal retirement life, highlighting the importance of planning your life with intention in setting goals and coordinating your decisions to your priorities and values. When you think about and design your retirement plans and goals, you will be able to build an exciting and meaningful life.

In the beginning, you need to consider your priorities and your priorities. Determine what's important for you when you retire and whether that's taking more time with your loved ones or pursuing your own interests or donating to cause or exploring new avenues. When you understand your primary goals and values that you will be able to make decisions based on your core values.

Determining what your retirement goals are the following stage. Create a vision and a description of your dream retirement life by looking at aspects like location, hobbies that you enjoy, your relationships, your personal development and the impact you make towards society. Think about how you would like to live your life and what gives you happiness and satisfaction. The vision you create can serve as a compass to help guide your decisions and actions.

When planning your retirement plan you must take into consideration the financial aspects. Consider how your vision for retirement is in line with your goals and financial resources. Be sure your choices in lifestyle can be sustained within your budget and you have a strategy in the place to help you maintain your ideal way of life in your retirement.

Wellness and health are essential to retiring. Make sure you take care of your mental, physical and emotional health by ensuring a healthy and balanced life. Get active regularly make positive friendships and develop lifestyles that help you achieve overall health. An active mind and body can make for a satisfying retirement.

Retirement provides the opportunity to indulge in your own interest and passions. Enjoy the opportunity to discover the new areas of interest, develop new techniques, and participate with activities that give your satisfaction as well as satisfaction. Continuous learning, inspiration as well as personal development are the key elements of an enjoyable retirement.

The theme of adventure and travel is often as a major part of retirement goals. Explore different types of travel as well as destinations that fit your preferences and financial budget. If you're interested in exploring far-flung regions, experiencing different world cultures, or taking part in thrilling adventures, traveling could be an transformative and enriching in retirement.

Establishing and maintaining relationships is a crucial aspect in creating your ideal retirement life. Maintain and cultivate connections with your family, friends as well as communities. Take part in social events or volunteer activities, as well as connect with groups of people who share similar passions. Relationships that are meaningful provide the feeling of belonging and can enhance the retirement.

Giving back and volunteering can contribute to a positive your retirement. Make use of your expertise, skills and time to support the causes that matter for your. Volunteering or helping charitable causes will allow you to have an impact that is positive and create satisfaction and fulfillment.

Making your dream early retirement life requires you to find an equilibrium between flexibility and structure. Set goals, create routines and keep a feeling of purpose, while also embracing flexibility and spontaneity. adjust to the new possibilities. You should be able to change your plan and priorities as the circumstances change.

When you begin to design your ideal retirement plan be aware that it's an ongoing process of change and change. Be open to opportunities, accept change and adjust as needed throughout the process. Retirement allows you to experiment and redefine yourself and allow your life to change as you go along.

The final step is to design the ideal early retirement life is an essential step toward creating a satisfying and meaningful life. Reflecting on the values you hold and defining your ideal retirement plan and weighing the financial implications placing a high value on health and well-being as well as pursuing interests that are personal to you as well as fostering relationships, taking part in volunteering as well as finding the perfect equilibrium, you will be able to create an ideal retirement life that gives satisfaction, fulfillment and satisfaction. Engage in actively making your retirement a success, and take advantage of the opportunities you'll encounter on the road to the early retirement you've always wanted.

Chapter 14: Health Insurance And Early Retirement

Insurance for health is an essential element of protecting your well-being financially and in your health when you are in the early stages of retirement. In this article we will discuss the significance of having health insurance during the early years of retirement. We also provide tips on how to navigate the complexities of healthcare in order to obtain the right protection. Through understanding the needs of your health as well as exploring your options in healthcare as well as staying up-to-date with new policies, you are able to take informed choices and safeguard yourself against unexpected medical costs.

The early retirement phase calls to carefully evaluate your health demands. Check your current health and anticipated medical expenses medical conditions that are pre-existing, prescription drugs and other lifestyle variables. Being aware of your medical needs allows you to choose the most appropriate insurance choices and plan for future cost.

If you previously had coverage by an employer-sponsored insurance plan, COBRA (Consolidated Omnibus Budget Reconciliation Act) provides temporary coverage for continuation. Examine the length of coverage, eligibility criteria, and the cost of COBRA coverage in order to bridge gaps until you can find an appropriate permanent option.

Options for health insurance prior to Medicare access vary based upon your specific circumstances. Consider private health insurance plans and health sharing programs, and health insurance for short-term duration to discover coverage that fits the needs of your family. Be aware of the pros and cons and prices of every choice is essential to make the right choice.

The Affordable Health Care Act (ACA) has had a significant impact on the landscape of healthcare. Discover more about healthcare exchanges, and how to avail subsidies and tax credit for those who are early retiring. Health exchanges provide the ability to choose from a variety of health insurance policies knowing the different options of coverage as well as costs that come with each plan is essential to find the right options for coverage.

Medicare plays an important role when it comes to healthcare coverage for retirees. Know the eligibility requirements and how to apply for Medicare. Learn about the various components of Medicare which include Parts A B, C and D. You can also look into coverage options that are in alignment with your health needs.

You should consider Medicare Advantage plans (Part C) and Medigap policies (Supplemental Medicare plans) to help you supplement or enhance the benefits of your Medicare coverage. These plans fill in the holes in Medicare coverage, and provide more benefits.

Insurance for long-term care is a crucial aspect to consider for those who are early retiring. Learn about the benefits and costs of long-term care insurance policies. They provide insurance for long-term health services that are not paid for by health insurance or Medicare.

Health Savings Accounts (HSAs) as well as Flexible Spending Accounts (FSAs) provide tax-friendly options to invest in medical costs. Check out these options and be aware of the limits on contributions, eligibility costs, as well as the tax benefits that they can provide.

Be aware of changes to health policies and rules. When healthcare legislation changes is important to know the potential impact of changes on the coverage you have and cost. Keep up-to-date with trustworthy sources and seek expert assistance when needed.

Preparing for the possibility of unexpected medical expenses is essential. Make sure you have funds set aside specifically for healthcare expenses. You can also plan for unexpected medical emergencies. Being aware of your insurance coverage and the costs out of pocket helps you plan for unforeseen events.

Talking to healthcare and insurance professionals could provide helpful advice on the murky waters of healthcare insurance. Insurance brokers, financial advisors and health experts are able to assist you in assessing your options, comprehend the fine print and make educated decisions.

Conclusion: securing the health insurance you need is an essential part of early retirement planning. When you evaluate your needs for healthcare by examining various options for coverage and understanding the latest policy developments as well as seeking advice from a professional to protect your financial and health when you retire early. Make a conscious effort to plan your healthcare, prioritize healthcare insurance and be sure you're covered enough for a satisfying and stress-free retirement.

Chapter 15: Relocation And Geographic Arbitrage

The concept of geographic arbitrage and relocation plays crucial roles when it comes to achieving financial freedom and the possibility of early retirement. In this section we examine the value in making a strategically choice and explore the idea of geographic arbitrage. This will maximize your earnings as well as savings. Through analyzing potential places and weighing the financial implications as well as embracing the potential which come from moving, you will be able to create your ideal lifestyle, which is compatible with your ambitions and goals.

In the event of a relocation plan It is crucial to assess possible destinations on the basis of a variety of aspects. Consider the costs of living, the quality of life, health options tax rates, climate in addition to the proximity of your family and close friends. Every factor affects the general suitability and desirableness of the location you choose for your early retirement.

Considerations regarding finances play an important influence on the decision to move. Consider the costs of living at your present location against potential locations. Assess the cost of living tax, the cost of living, and possible savings opportunities in regions with less expensive living costs. The move to an area that has less expensive living costs could significantly increase your earnings and save you money, speeding up the process of becoming financially independent.

Geographic arbitrage, an important concept of early retirement allows you to maximize your income through moving to an area where living costs are lower. When you make a profit more than your price of living locally and thereby saving money in the long run, make more investments, and have a better quality of living. The concept of geographic arbitrage is particularly useful for remote employees as well as entrepreneurs and those working from a mobile location.

Explore different housing options that you could consider in different locations. Consider buying, renting, or downsizing your home based on your budget and personal preferences. Examine real estate issues like property prices rent yields, property values, and the likelihood of the appreciation of your property. The cost of housing is often the majority of your expenditure while a careful analysis could help you make more informed decision.

Making the transition to a new place is a crucial aspect of moving. Make the most of your opportunity to establish an entirely new network of friends as well as explore local resources as well as integrate into the neighborhood. Get involved in local activities and join organizations or clubs that foster relationships for a satisfying and active social life the new place you've chosen to live in.

The rapid growth of remote work opens the door to greater the freedom of location. The digital nomads and those who work remotely can work anywhere and from any location, allowing the flexibility to choose the location of their next move. Take advantage of the benefits of remote working and take into consideration what opportunities it can bring to the early retirement you've always dreamed of.

International relocation provides unique options but it also comes with other considerations. Examine visa requirements, healthcare system, language barriers as well as cultural changes when thinking about an international move. Traveling abroad can provide exciting experiences, cultural variety, and may even less expensive living costs However, a thorough planning is vital.

Moving places can affect not just your financial situation but also general quality of living. Take into consideration factors like the outdoors, accessibility to facilities, cultural options and involvement with the community at potential destinations. Achieving a balance between life style and financial goals can ensure that you have a pleasant and satisfying beginning your retirement.

Relocating is a meticulous process that requires planning and organization. Make plans for expenses related to moving such as finding a new home, moving utilities, and creating new routines. Make a checklist and timeline for a smooth transition into your new home.

Moving is a type of investment that will yield substantial returns. Examine the return on investment (ROI) of moving with regard to saving money, improvement in quality of life, as well as personal satisfaction. It could help achieve financial security as well as early retirement objectives by maximizing your spending and ensuring a life that matches your beliefs and goals.

Be aware of personal and family aspects when making relocation choices. Take into account the wants and requirements of your family members, considering their needs as well as the potential impact they could have upon their daily lives. Honest and transparent communication is essential to ensure that any relocation plan is based on the health and well-being of all those affected.

Also, remember the need for flexibility in the long run. The preferences and conditions may shift in time. Be open to the possibility of adapting or make changes and possibly relocate in the future when it's in alignment with your changing objectives and goals.

Relocation as well as geographic arbitrage can provide you with the chance to maximize your financial situation as well as enhance your living as well as accelerate your progress toward financial freedom and the early retirement. Through analyzing possible locations taking into consideration financial implications and embracing the possibilities offered by remote work as well as balancing personal considerations and financial considerations, you can create a satisfying and fulfilling retirement plan. Take advantage of the opportunities that come from moving, and build your life in alignment with your goals and dreams.

Chapter 16: Post-Fire Considerations
Sustainable Withdrawal Strategies

When you move from the accumulation phase into the withdrawal phase during the early stages of retirement, managing your financial situation becomes an important factor to take into. Chapter 16 examines the post-FIRE phase and concentrates on strategies for a sustainable withdrawal to make sure you have a long-lasting investment portfolio as well as ensure your financial stability during retirement. Through understanding the withdrawal rate as well as analyzing your financial requirements and then implementing a strategy that is effective that will help you deal with the challenges and difficulties that come with post-FIRE.

It is crucial to comprehend the notion of viable withdrawal rates. The 4percent rule, which is widely used as a guideline recommends that you withdraw 4percent of the initial investment value, adjusted to inflation every year is most likely to provide an income that is sustainable over a period of at least 30 years. But, it's important to analyze your financial requirements and plans to determine the appropriate withdrawal amount that would be better suited to the specific situation.

Examining your financial requirements and objectives post-FIRE is crucial. Take into consideration your expected expenditures, your desired lifestyle as well as potential medical expenses and other income sources. Analyzing these aspects allows you to decide on a withdrawal plan that is compatible with your personal financial needs and goals.

Although the 4percent rule is a popular one however, there are other withdrawal methods. Consider the method of variable percentage withdrawal that adjusts the each year's withdrawals in accordance with how your portfolio performs, as well as the bucket method and is a method of dividing your portfolio into several buckets that have different degrees of risk and levels of liquidity. Learning about different withdrawal strategies will assist you in making an informed choice based on your level of risk and your income requirements.

Allocation of assets to portfolios and managing risk are important aspects to consider during withdrawal. In the long run, balancing income and growth while diversifying investments and reducing risk are essential to ensure your portfolio's stability for the long-term. Making adjustments to your asset allocation when you shift from an accumulation phase towards the withdrawal phase could aid in maintaining a healthy and sustainable strategy for investing.

Tax-related considerations play an important influence on withdrawal strategies. Consider tax-efficient investments by prioritizing tax-free accounts. Also, think about Roth conversions in order to maximize efficiency in taxation. Through strategically managing your tax affairs it will reduce taxes and increase the life span of your investment portfolio.

Making adjustments to your withdrawal rate in line with inflation is a crucial element of the withdrawal strategies post-FIRE. As inflation increases, purchasing power decreases with time Therefore, it's crucial to think about how you can take into account inflation, and then adjust the withdrawal rates accordingly. Using a plan to ensure that your money is kept up with the rate of inflation can help keep your lifestyle comfortable through retirement.

The risk of sequence of returns is a crucial consideration during the process of withdrawing. The timing that you receive the return on your investment can have a significant impact on your investment's longevity. You can reduce this risk by diversifying your investment portfolio and using the concept of a bond tent (increasing the amount of bonds you hold near retirement) in addition to creating cash reserves that can endure market declines without having to sell your investments in the loss.

The risk of longevity, also known as the chance of living beyond the savings you have saved for retirement, must be taken into consideration when preparing your withdrawal strategy. You should think about contingency planning for example, generating extra income from part-time jobs or even lowering expenses in the event of a need. Making a strategy for addressing unexpected events will ensure that you are prepared to deal with any financial issues which may occur.

The monitoring and adjustment of the withdrawal plan is crucial in the course of your post-FIRE years. Keep yourself informed of the market's conditions and monitor the performance of your portfolio and frequently review your goals for financial success. By being proactive about review of your strategies lets you make changes to ensure financial stability. Consulting with a professional will provide invaluable insights in the post-FIRE period. Financial planners, financial advisors and specialists in their field can assist to navigate the withdrawal process and improve your financial position. Their knowledge and expertise will provide assurance and make sure you take well-informed decision-making.

Finally, managing your financial situation post-FIRE requires focus on the psychological and emotional aspects. Being financially confident, reducing anxiety and finding a an equilibrium in your pursuit of financial independence as well as early retirement is crucial. Be aware of your own self, get help in times of need, and keep your eyes on having a satisfying and meaningful retirement.

The conclusion is that life after FIRE demands careful thought about viable withdrawal strategies that will ensure an income that is secure throughout retirement. If you are aware of the rates for withdrawal and assessing your needs in terms of financial and devising strategies that work to manage your finances, you will be able to deal with the challenges of managing your financial affairs during this time. Keep an eye on your finances, be flexible to changes in your life and seek advice from a professional in order to live your secure and satisfying life post-FIRE.

Chapter 17: Managing Risks And Contingencies

Examines the vital issue of managing risk and contingencies during early retirement Even though early retirement provides the opportunity to pursue your interests and live your life according to your own terms but it is important to recognize and manage dangers that could threaten your financial security and wellbeing. If you are aware of the risks involved and implementing strategies for managing risk as well as having prepared contingency plans to manage risks and have a more safe and secure early retirement.

In the beginning, it's crucial to determine and evaluate the potential risks early retirees could be facing. This could include fluctuations in the market and inflation, health costs as well as longevity risks and unanticipated expenses. If you are aware of these risks and the potential consequences they could have on your financial position it is possible to develop strategies to reduce and control them efficiently.

Diversification and asset allocation are crucial to managing risk in investment. The diversification of your portfolio over different types of assets can reduce the effects of market volatility and reduce the risks associated to the individual investment. If you spread your investment across diverse sectors, regions as well as asset classes could help boost return while decreasing risks.

Insurance coverage is an additional component of risk-management. Insurance for life, health insurance, disability insurance as well as long-term care insurance, are essential tools for protecting you and your family members from financial hardships that may arise. Review your insurance requirements and be sure that you have enough coverage in order to reduce the risk of the cost of medical bills as well as loss of income as well as other unexpected circumstances.

Maintaining emergency cash as well as cash reserves is vital in coping with sudden expenses and interruptions in income. Make sure you have a minimum of three months' worth daily expenses available through liquid assets. These assets provide an insurance policy when you are in financial trouble and help you navigate unpredictable financial challenges without compromising the stability of your financial future.

The risk of longevity, or the possibility of not living up to the retirement savings that you've made, needs to be considered with care. Consider your expected life span and take into consideration the possibility of health costs during retirement. Create a plan for how you will cover the costs and consider alternatives like long-term care insurance, which can protect you against the rising healthcare costs later on in the course of your.

Planning for your estate is essential for ensuring the seamless transfer of wealth, and to ensure your assets are protected for the next generations. Make a complete estate plan, which includes wills, trusts and powers of attorney and beneficiary designations. Review and regularly modify your estate plan in order to reflect changes regarding your personal circumstances or wishes.

Planning for contingencies is essential to managing unexpected income losses or shifts in income when you are near retirement. Take into consideration options such as taking part-time jobs and passive income streams and even adjusting your expenses as needed. This flexible strategy put in place lets you change your financial situation and ensure the stability of your finances.

Examine and evaluate your risk management plans regularly. Review regularly the efficacy of your contingency plans policies for insurance, as well as your investments. Modify your plans as required to make sure they are in line with your objectives and current economic as well as personal environment.

The management of risks and contingencies requires addressing the psychological as well as emotional implications of the uncertainty. The early retirement phase can cause fears and anxieties however, gaining the ability to overcome challenges, seeking out support and keeping a positive attitude can assist in navigating these difficulties.

the advice of a professional is essential to manage risks and unforeseen events effectively. Financial advisers, estate planners and insurance experts are able to provide professional advice and guidance. They can help to create a complete strategy for managing risk that is tailored to the specific requirements of your business.

As a result, taking care of risks and contingencies is essential for success in your early retirement. When you identify risks, using the right strategies as well as having contingency plans put implemented, you are able to manage uncertainties and have an enjoyable and secure retirement. Make sure you prioritize risk management. Regularly examine your strategies, consult with a professional whenever needed, to guarantee solid financial security as well as peace of mind when you enter the early years of retirement.

Chapter 18: Nurturing Relationships In Early Retirement

Focuses on the significance of maintaining relationships during the early years of retirement Although financial freedom as well as personal fulfillment are both important objectives but the relationship quality plays an important role for our general well-being and overall happiness. In this section we will explore ways of consolidating existing relationships, forming new ones, reuniting with those we love and interacting with the wider community. Through prioritizing connections early retirees will feel more fulfilled and have an increased sense of belonging the new phase of their lives.

The ability to maintain strong relationships between family members, partners and friends from the past is crucial in the early years of retirement. A good communication system, spending time time together and fostering common experiences are a great way to nurture and build these bonds. Make sure to have honest and open conversations, pay attention to one another and try to stay connected.

Establishing new relationships and sustaining ones you have already made can be a significant part of your experience in retirement. Take part in a variety of activities and interests which align with your interests. Join clubs or social associations Be proactive when making connections with friends. Find opportunities to connect with new people, participate in social events in your community, and build relationships which provide each other with support and sharing experience.

Connecting with family members who were distant throughout the course of your career can be a chance to rekindle and build friendships. Contact your family, friends or people with whom have lost contact. Develop deeper bonds by putting in time and energy into maintaining these connections. Tell stories, talk about past experiences and make fresh memories.

Community involvement and volunteering provide a valuable opportunity to give back to society as well as fostering connections with others. Think about committing your time and expertise to organizations or causes that reflect your ideals and passions. Volunteering is not just beneficial to communities but it also gives the opportunity to connect with like-minded people and develop new relationships.

Achieving a balance of time for personal time as well as social interaction is crucial in the early years of retirement. Although it is essential to find time to reflect on your life or hobbies as well as private pursuits, being engaged with your friends is also essential. Find a way to balance your time that permits the pursuit of your own passions and still be active in activities with friends that provide satisfaction and a sense of connection.

Cultural and travel experiences are also a great way to strengthen relationships, expanding horizons and allowing to share experiences. Experience new locations, learn about various cultures, and connect with people from the area. Traveling is not just a way to expand your knowledge of the world, but can make lasting memories with your loved ones and new acquaintances that you make on the way.

The nurturing of relationships between generations can be rewarding and uplifting. Engage with the younger generation including grandchildren, children, or nephews and nieces for a chance to connect generations and exchange knowledge and experience. Learn from them and form strong bonds with the different ages.

A strong relationship with your partner or creating new romantic bonds is another way to nurture relationships during early retirement. The ability to communicate, the emotional connection and sharing activities are the most important elements in creating a satisfying romantic partnership. Make sure you invest time and energy in sustaining an emotional bond with your spouse and discover different ways to increase the intimacy of your relationship and increase mutual relationship.

Groups of support and peer networks are essential to early retirement. Find a group of like-minded people that understand your dreams and obstacles. Join community groups and support groups that allow you to exchange experiences, get advice and provide each other with support during the path to financial freedom and the early retirement you've always wanted.

Technology also aids in relationships in the early years of retirement. Make use of social media as well as video calls and social networks to stay in touch to family and friends that may live far away. Make use of technology to build relationships and remain in touch despite distances.

The ability to manage conflicts and issues that can arise from relationships is essential to maintain good relationships. Learn effective communication techniques by practicing active listening and develop strategies for resolving conflicts. Respecting the boundaries of healthy behavior is crucial for building positive relationships.

Think about your legacy and the effects you'd like to leave behind on the relationships you have with your community. Transfer wisdom, knowledge as well as life lessons for the future generation. Make a lasting impression through giving back to the community and inspiring the next generation.

To conclude, maintaining connections is an essential part of the early years of retirement. If you invest time and energy into strengthening existing connections, establishing new ones, connecting with your loved ones and being involved in the communities, you'll enjoy greater satisfaction and feeling of belonging. Make time for relationships, engage in important interactions and develop an unwavering network of friends that can enrich your journey to early retirement.

Chapter 19: Finding Purpose And Meaning After Retirement

The significance of finding meaning and meaning when you retire While leisure and financial independence are important aspects of retiring but a sense of purpose and significance is just as important for the overall wellbeing and satisfaction. In this section we look at strategies for taking stock of your personal values, interests and hobbies, involving in ongoing learning, volunteer and community service, entrepreneurial in pursuit of passion-driven projects and interests, mentorship as well as embracing wellness and health traveling and exploring cultures and environmental projects, establishing connections, spiritual practice in philanthropy, as well as the importance of balancing various avenues of meaning. Through these approaches retired people will find a renewed sense of motivation and an underlying feeling of satisfaction during this exciting new chapter of their lives.

It is crucial to assess your personal interests, values and hobbies. Think about what's important for you and what is bringing your joy. Making sure your retirement plans are in line with these elements can give you a the most profound sense of purpose and satisfaction. If it's engaging in creative pursuits and promoting causes you are passionate about, or taking part in activities that align with your values of the heart, getting in line to your values can be a great approach to inject meaning into your retirement.

The pursuit of continual growing and learning can be an additional way to find what is important and meaningful. Being involved in pursuits of knowledge as well as acquiring knowledge and gaining new skills could provide satisfaction and provide new possibilities. Discover topics and hobbies that always enticed you. You can also enroll in classes or join study groups to challenge your intellect and promote your personal development.

Volunteering and service to the community are rewarding ways of making an impact on the lives of others and find meaning in your retiring. Spend your time as well as your skills and experience to cause or organization which resonate with you. Giving back to your community does will not only benefit others, but it also gives you an inner sense of purpose and a sense of connection.

Inspiring yourself to be an entrepreneur and launching your own business could provide the sense of fulfillment and a new challenge after retirement. Find opportunities to explore entrepreneurial endeavors, or transform your interests into lucrative business ventures. Beginning a new business allows the use of your abilities and knowledge while generating something that is meaningful and satisfying.

Hobbies and passion projects can be powerful ways to find the purpose and significance. Participate in activities that give your heart to the ground, whether that's writing, painting, gardening or another creative activity. The activities you choose to engage in could provide an experience of satisfaction as well as personal expression and an increased feeling of meaning.

The sharing of knowledge with other people is an effective method to gain an end-to-end purpose in your the years of retirement. Share your knowledge as well as your skills and knowledge to the next generation. Get involved with the younger generation by mentoring programmes, education initiatives or other community-based organizations. You can leave a lasting impression by helping other people be successful.

Health and wellness is crucial to find purpose and meaning when you retire. Be active and regularly exercise as well as adopt healthy lifestyle choices as well as prioritize taking care of yourself. If you take charge of your physical as well as mental wellbeing, you'll feel more energetic and energized to live your life and live a life of purpose.

The world of travel and exploration provide an opportunity to grow personally in self-discovery, discovery, as well as finding purpose during retirement. Discover new destinations as well as immerse yourself into different culture, and connect with your local communities. The experiences expand your perspectives as well as foster compassion and provide a new perspective about the world around you.

Being involved in environmental efforts can help retirees contribute to the sustainability of our future. Help causes that are related to environmental conservation, sustainable practices, or alternative energy sources. Through active participation in environmental projects and initiatives, you will create a positive change and create a more sustainable world for the future generation.

Establishing and maintaining relationships are crucial to find purpose and meaning during retirement. Spend time and time with friends and family and make meaningful connections with your local community, and create the development of a network of support. Relationships that are meaningful provide an underlying sense of connection as well as support and satisfaction.

The practice of mindfulness and meditation are able to provide an increased feeling of meaning and purpose. Try practices like yoga, meditation or other contemplative activities that help to promote internal peace, self-reflection and the ability to see clearly. The practice can foster feelings of meaning that transcend the material world.

Being involved in charitable giving and giving to society can be an effective way of finding the purpose and significance of retiring. Give back to charities, contribute to the community's development as well as make a difference in the lives of others. When you volunteer to the community, you will leave an enduring legacy that goes beyond your lifetime.

Finding balance between different avenues of pursuit is essential when you retire. Take advantage of a wide range of pursuits which align with your ideals or interests, as well as passions. The ability to balance personal pursuits, friendships with friends, interests, and social participation allows you to find satisfaction on many different levels.

Finding purpose and meaning when you retire is a personal and arduous process. Through analyzing your priorities, continuing to learn by volunteering, the pursuit of entrepreneurship, projects with passions as well as mentoring and environmental projects, traveling and building connections and spirituality, giving back as well as balancing multiple avenues of motivation, people who retire will find renewed satisfaction as well as a feeling of purpose during this exciting new stage of their lives. Enjoy the new opportunities retirement brings, pursue your interests, and build a life-long purpose that will bring satisfaction, joy as well as a lasting impression on you and your loved ones.

Chapter 20: Celebrating Financial Independence And Early Retirement

Financial independence journey and early retirement path It is a time to be proud of the successes and look forward to the next chapter in life which lies ahead. In this chapter we reflect about the experience, celebrate the achievements, plan retirement celebrations as well as share our experiences, acknowledge our gratitude, welcome fresh beginnings, create new goals and create a an indelible legacy. It's the perfect time to rejoice in the newfound liberty, recognize the difficult labor, and encourage other people to begin your own journey to the financial security and early retirement.

The process of reflecting on our journey can be an exercise that can help us to recognize how far we've come. Spend a few minutes reflecting about the struggles as well as the sacrifices and achievements which led us to where we are today. Consider the effort, dedication and persistence it took to reach financial freedom. Honor your achievements as well as your progress made on your journey.

Honoring achievements and success is a key element of celebrating financial independence and the possibility of early retirement. Be proud of the financial milestones that you've achieved, like the repayment of your debts, meeting your savings goals that you've always wanted to achieve or achieving investment goals. Be proud of your achievements as well as the financial independence that you've gained.

The idea of a retirement party can be a great opportunity to mark the passage to early retirement. Think about gathering with your loved ones and hosting a memorable celebration, or embarking on an exciting excursion. Enjoy the company of those who have accompanied you on your adventure. Make this an opportunity to thank them and to share your hopes in the near future.

The sharing of your story with others can be a great method to show gratitude. The journey you've taken to financial freedom and early retirement may inspire and encourage other people. Think about sharing your experience your lessons learnt, as well as your successes through speeches, writing or on online platforms. Encourage others to become more in control of their financial life and achieve their personal goals of a successful early retirement.

Being grateful is a crucial aspect of celebrating financial freedom as well as early retirement. Spend time to acknowledge all those who helped throughout your journey, whether family members, your friends and mentors or financial advisers. Show appreciation to them for their help confidence, support, and trust in your capability to attain financially independent. The act of gratitude strengthens relationships and promotes an attitude of positivity.

The opportunity to embrace new beginnings is an exciting part that comes with early retirement. Take advantage of the flexibility and freedom of financial freedom. Discover new hobbies, passions or business ventures that are in line with your values and interests. Take advantage of the chance to build a your own fulfilling, purpose-driven retirement living.

Making new aspirations and goals is an inevitable step when you are in the early stages of retirement. Always push yourself to improve by learning, gaining knowledge, and engage in exciting new ventures. Create goals that are meaningful and correspond with your beliefs and hopes for this phase of your life. It doesn't matter if it's acquiring something new, launching an innovative project or creating an impact in your neighborhood, aim for an ongoing sense of fulfillment for yourself.

A financially-skilled mindset is essential even when you are in an early stage of retirement. Keep your money and fortune by paying attention to the amount you spend, establishing an emergency fund as well as adjusting to the changing circumstances in the financial world. Take informed decisions regarding the cost of your investment and expenditures to guarantee your financial stability for the long term.

The ability to balance work and leisure is one of the most important aspects of the early years of retirement. Take advantage of your newfound time off time However, also look for reasons to participate in activities that are meaningful to you. Explore hobbies, help the causes you believe in by the act of volunteering or mentoring and explore work-from-home possibilities that are in line with your values and interests.

A lasting legacy can be the best way to create an impact that will be beneficial to those who come after you or your community. Think about ways to share the knowledge, skills or time for a long-lasting impression. Consider supporting causes that matter for you, donate to charities or help others want to be financially independent.

Celebrations of milestones and anniversary dates are the perfect opportunity to look back on your progress and successes achieved. Consider important dates for instance, the day when you reached financial independence, or the day you took the day you took early retirement. Make these dates a time to appreciate your accomplishments and also to make a dedication to a satisfying and meaningful life.

Joining those in the Financial Independence, Retire Early (FIRE) group can provide continuous support and motivation. Join with others who share similar interests via online forums, go to events, or join local gatherings. Talk about your experiences, get guidance, and gain knowledge from other people who are on the same path.

To conclude, the chapter 20 is an ideal time to commemorate the hard earned financial freedom and the early retirement. Reminisce about your journey and celebrate your accomplishments, organize celebrations, tell your story and express your gratitude. Also, welcome the new opportunities, establish objectives for the future, and leave a the legacy that will last forever. Enjoy this chapter in your life and encourage others to take the same way to financial freedom or early retirement. Enjoy the possibilities, freedom and possibilities that lie ahead. And live your an active and satisfying life.

Chapter 21: Embracing The New World Of Remote Work

The workplace is swiftly changing and the rapid growth of remote working opens up new opportunities to those who seek freedom in their work, flexibility and the ability to earn a living. The chapter will explore the advantages of remote work. we'll look at the advantages of remote working, and how to get around the remote employment market, how to set up an effective office at home, and develop the fundamental skills required to succeed in the remote workplace.

Section 1: The Benefits of Remote Work

Remote work has many advantages which have drawn people from different professional backgrounds. The most significant benefit is the freedom it offers. Remote workers are able to decide on their work time and place of work, which allows the possibility of a more balanced work/life. Remote working is often associated with higher productivity, due to the reduction of distractions, and also the capability to build a personalised workplace that maximizes concentration and productivity. Remote work may yield significant savings through the elimination of commuting costs and work-related clothing expenses as well as the requirement for an office space.

Section 2: Navigating the Remote Job Market

The search for remote-based job opportunities demands an organized approach. Begin by looking through reliable job boards, specific to remote work websites, as well as freelance sites. They offer a broad selection of jobs that are remote in various industries. Making sure you tailor your cover letter and resume to showcase your remote working expertise, pertinent skills as well as your ability to work in a team is vital. You should consider creating a portfolio online or website to show off your skills and demonstrate the remote capabilities you have. Joining remote work groups or networking events may provide valuable connections as well as career opportunities.

Section 3: Setting Up Your Home Office

Setting up a workspace that is dedicated to the home environment is essential to successful remote working. Pick a place that is peaceful and with no distractions, and set the space in a manner that encourages productivity and comfort. Consider investing on ergonomic chairs and tools to help you maintain a good posture and lessen the strain on your body. Create your own routine which is in line with your best hours of productivity and establishes a clear line between personal and work. It is important to establish limits with your family members or roommates, and creating a regular routine. It's true that this second part isn't easy because your spouse's kids or parents may not be familiar with the Work-from-home mentality and might be tempted to dismiss it as a matter that doesn't require the same level of focus like a job in a company. Be aware that you are the person who is responsible for providing your dedication and do the work to ensure it benefits you.

Section 4: Effective Communication and Collaboration

Effective and clear communication is essential for remote workers. Make use of communication tools, such as video conferencing software and instant messaging applications and software for managing projects to remain in contact with your colleagues and customers, in case your direction calls for the use of these tools. Engage in active participation in online meetings, participate with active listening and share ideas that can foster cooperation. Making connections remotely requires a lot of work. Take part in online team-building events or schedule informal video conferences to meet colleagues, and take part in professional online communities that help you expand your circle of friends. If I say "colleagues" this doesn't mean "colleagues" in the sense of corporate employees. They could be the people that you work with for a brief task, such as creating music for an artist or publishing a book. All of these requires a team effort.

Section 5: Developing Remote Work Skills

Succeeding in remote work requires developing essential skills. Dedication, time management and discipline are essential for being focused and completing deadlines. Establish clear objectives prioritizing tasks and develop an established routine to help you control your time efficiently. Flexibility and problem-solving are vital for navigating through the obstacles which may occur when working remote. Learn to come up with creative ideas, discover new solutions, and be able to adapt to changes in the environment. Take advantage of ongoing training and professional development through taking advantage of online classes, webinars and other resources from the industry to improve your abilities and keep current with the latest the latest trends in remote work. It is important to note that not all online courses will be useful for the individual, so conduct your own research ahead of time and avoid spending your cash in a course promising quick riches. It is recommended to take courses that help you improve yourself or to learn new skills at accredited organizations like universities offering this type of course. Other great places you can get certified for on-demand skills are classcentral.com and learndigital.withgoogle.com for free. The way I would recommend it is: Begin by making your list of all your hobbies that you enjoy or are interested in learning about. Choose the top three from this list, and then do the necessary research to determine where you could improve your skills. One of the main reasons to work at home is doing things you're enthusiastic about. It isn't like working since you're truly enjoying your work, isn't it? To me, the concept of creativity was something that I've always leaned towards. So naturally, my initial step to do something with meaning for me was to sign to the Graphic Design program.

Conclusion The chapter we discussed the benefits of remote working, methods to get through the remote jobs market as well as setting up an efficient work space at home, and learning the essential skills for remote work. Remote work can provide greater flexibility, higher productivity and savings on costs, making it a desirable choice for people looking to explore an alternative method of working. When you implement the methods described in this section, you'll be prepared to begin your journey to work remotely and prepare yourself for success in the rapidly changing realm of remote working and self-employment.

Chapter 22: Identifying Lucrative Opportunities In The Digital Space

In this section we'll look at the various income streams that are available online. From freelancers and e-commerce affiliate marketing and online training We will explore every opportunity's possibilities and provide an example to help learn how to be successful.

Section 1: Freelancing

It is a way to be self-employed and offers an array of options. If, for instance, you're a skilled writer and are able to provide the creation of content, copywriting or editing. If you excel in graphic design, you can provide logo design, branding, or website design services. Platforms such as Upwork, Freelancer, and Fiverr provide freelancers with customers who are looking for specific talents. Through creating a captivating profile, showing off your work portfolio and providing quality work, you will make clients want to hire you and establish an impressive freelance business.

Section 2: E-commerce

The popularity of online shopping has increased and allows individuals to market items on the internet. If, for instance, you love jewellery made by hand, you may start an online shop on platforms such as Shopify and Etsy. With a well-designed site, enhancing product descriptions featuring appealing descriptions and top-quality photos, while also providing exceptional customer support, you are able to bring in customers and drive sales. Make use of social media marketing to work with influential people in your area, and utilize SEO techniques for directing targeted traffic towards your website store.

Section 3: Affiliate Marketing

Affiliate marketing allows you to earn commissions from marketing other offerings or products. If, for instance, you have a passion for fitness, then you may want to start a blog or a website that provide useful content like workout routines as well as healthy food recipes and review of products. If you sign up to affiliate programs from fitness-related brands, you will be able to endorse their products and earn an income for every sale generated through your exclusive affiliate hyperlink. Make use of social media as well as email marketing campaigns as well as search engine optimization techniques to broaden your reach and increase your earnings from affiliates.

Section 4: Online Courses

The need for online education is increasing, making online learning a profitable business. In the case of instance, if you're an experienced photographer, you may be able to make an online photography class. The course can be divided into segments that will cover a variety of topics like camera methods as well as composition and editing. Create your course and host it through platforms such as Udemy or Teachable and promote it to a worldwide public. Make learning more enjoyable with videos, interactive questions and offering ongoing assistance for your students. Make use of marketing methods such as content marketing, promotion of social media as well as collaborations with experts from other fields within the field to bring students to your class.

Section 5: Dropshipping

Dropshipping offers a low-risk method to begin an online business with no inventory to hold. For instance, let's say you find an item that is trending for example, like blenders that are portable. Make a deal with reputable suppliers and create your own online store on platforms such as Shopify. Upload the listings of products and concentrate on writing appealing product descriptions that are high-quality and have attractive photographs. When a client makes an order, the vendor will handle the fulfillment and shipment directly to the purchaser. Use social media ads or influencer partnerships, as well as search engine optimization to bring shoppers to your site and increase sales. Monitor trends and preference to increase your product options and keep one step ahead of the pack.

Section 6: Cryptocurrency and Blockchain

Blockchain and cryptocurrency technology has transformed the world of finance providing unique opportunities to people who are interested in the digital area. Consider buying cryptocurrencies such as Bitcoin, Ethereum, or Litecoin. Learn the basics and market developments, use reputable cryptocurrency exchanges to purchase or sell digital assets. It is also possible to investigate the idea of mining cryptocurrencies or even staking them in order to earn an income that is passive. Be informed of new developments and information in the world of blockchain technology to find investment opportunities as well as new blockchain-based applications that are innovative in different areas, such as health, finance, or the management of supply chains.

Conclusion The conclusion of this chapter is that we looked at a variety of profitable opportunities within the online space. The e-commerce industry, freelancing and affiliate marketing, as well as dropshipping, online classes and crypto, as well as blockchain are all unique and have distinct benefits and the potential to be successful. Through leveraging the right platforms, strategies for marketing, and advancing your knowledge to create an online business that is profitable. Be sure to look for possibilities that are in line with your strengths, interests, as well as your long-term objectives. If you are proactive and adapting to the changing landscape of digital technology and opportunities, you will be able to begin a rewarding journey of earning cash from your at home.

Chapter 23: Building Your Online Presence And Personal Brand

The digital world is advancing rapidly, and having a solid web presence and establishing an identity for yourself is crucial to be successful. In chapter 3 "From 9 to 5 to Freedom: How to Earn the money you want from your home by 2023" we'll dive into the intricate process of building an effective web presence that is a hit with the people you want to reach. If you follow the guidelines in the chapter, you can create a brand that is memorable that will attract customers, clients as well as opportunities.

Section 1: Defining Your Brand Identity

Define your brand's image is the basis of your web presence. The first step is to identify your key value, distinctive strengths, and what value you can provide to your visitors. Take into consideration your audience as well as the emotion you hope to inspire from your audience. Create a mission statement that conveys your mission and branding story that connects your target audience on a personal scale. Your story should reflect your personal journey, the obstacles that you've conquered, as well as the changes you're able to aid your followers to reach. Find a tone of voice for your brand that is a reflection of your character and is a match for the ideal customers or clients. Are you knowledgeable and professional? Fun and likable? Are you consistent in your messages? Determine the tone and style that you'll use in your communication with your target audience.

Section 2: Creating a Professional Website

Your website is the center of your web presence. This is the chance to give a powerful first impression and show off your business. Choose an appropriate domain name with your company's image and then choose a reliable domain registrar. Make use of website builders such as WordPress, Wix, or Squarespace to build an appealing, user-friendly and visually pleasing site. Make sure your site is well-organized with clear directions, captivating content and captivating visuals. Add an About page that tells the story of your business and connects with the audience emotionally.

Highlight your product or service products, and highlight the advantages and solutions that they provide. Use testimonials, case studies or other examples to increase trust and establish credibility. Make a contact page which lets visitors contact you for inquiries or partnerships. Make your site more search-friendly for engines by conducting keyword searches by optimising meta tags and description in addition to ensuring your website is responsive to mobile devices. Make sure your website is regularly updated with the latest articles, blog posts or updates on news to keep your visitors interested.

Section 3: Leveraging Social Media Platforms

Social media platforms can be powerful instruments for increasing your internet presence, and connecting with the people you want to reach. Find the most appropriate platforms to your specific niche and audience, like Facebook, Instagram, Twitter, LinkedIn, or Pinterest. Make sure your profiles are consistent and engaging that are consistent with your branding image. Utilize top-quality cover and profile images that communicate your company's messages visually. Design a social media content plan that features an array of relevant images, informative content as well as relevant updates from the industry. Blog posts video or infographics which provide information and address your target audience's issues. Engage your audience via comments, likes and shares, by inviting questions or hosting contests. Utilize social media analytics to measure your results and get insights about your customers' preferences. Modify your strategies accordingly for maximum participation and the reach of your posts.

Section 4: Producing Valuable Content

Creation of content is an essential element of establishing your online image and earning credibility. Choose the type of content that is popular with your audience like blog posts, videos, podcasts or infographics. Create a calendar of content to keep a regular publishing schedule. Find out and tackle your audience's issues, pain points and aspirations of your target audience. Provide valuable information, useful advice, or step-by-step instructions for solving their challenges. Make your content search-friendly for engines through conducting keyword research and then incorporating keywords that are relevant within your posts. This increases the likelihood that your content will be discovered by your intended audience. Inspire engagement of your audience by including call-to-actions that encourage people to comment and ask questions or provide feedback. React quickly to comments or inquiries, thereby fostering the feeling of connectedness and confidence in your viewers.

Section 5: Engaging in Thought Leadership

Making yourself an expert within your field sets your business apart from others and makes you an authority. Offer your insight through several avenues, like hosting guest blogs, public speaking and participating at industry-related events. Find reputable websites or publications accepting guest blog posts. You can offer unique and interesting ideas for content. Invite yourself to be a speaker at events, webinars or podcasts in order to show off your expertise and knowledge. Join discussions through social media sites or forums that are specific to your industry, offering insightful insights and stimulating perspectives. Work with other influencers and experts within your field to increase your reach, and connect with their followers. Join interviews or feature podcasts to showcase your knowledge and connect with new audiences. Always provide valuable and informative information that makes you an authority in your field.

Final Conclusion The chapter 3 concluded that we looked at the specific ways to create a powerful web presence and develop an identity that is a hit with the people you want to reach. The creation of your brand's image and creating a professional site and leveraging the social networks, creating quality content and participating by expressing your thoughts are key components to create an effective online presence. If you implement these methods and continuously delivering quality content to your followers You will develop an impressive following, draw customers or clients and establish yourself as an expert in your field. In the following chapter we'll go over specific methods to make use of social media to gain the success of your business.

Chapter 24: Leveraging Social Media For Business Success

Platforms for social networking have revolutionized our way of connecting with each other, exchange information, and run our businesses. When you understand the distinct features of each one and using effective strategies you can increase brand recognition and engage your customers as well as drive more growth for your business from home.

Section 1: Choosing the Right Social Media Platforms

All social media platforms have the same features, so it is crucial to select ones that match the audience you want to reach and your company ambitions. Be aware of the demographics and needs of the people you want to reach. If, for instance, your customers are younger professionals, then platforms such LinkedIn or Twitter might be more efficient. If you're a visual artist with products, platforms such as Instagram or Pinterest are able to showcase them efficiently. Facebook is an incredibly flexible platform that has a large users. Pick the two or three platforms that will best fit the demographic you want to reach and concentrate your efforts to the ones that appeal to them.

Section 2: Developing a Social Media Strategy

A clearly defined plan for your social media presence is vital to make the most of the platforms. Begin by setting goals for your online presence. Are you looking to boost branding awareness, boost visitors to your website, increase leads or increase sales? Find out who your audience is and develop buyer personas in order to identify their interests, needs as well as their pain points. Create a distinctive benefit that sets you apart from the competition. Plan a strategy for your content which is consistent with the brand's identity and meets the needs of your target audience. Utilize a mixture of educational fun, educational, and promotional material. Use visual elements like pictures and videos or infographics to attract the attention of your audience. Set up a schedule for posting to ensure consistent and regular participation.

3. Engaging Your audience

Social media is about creating relationships and encouraging interaction with your followers. Answer messages, comments or mentions quickly and in a way that is personalized. Engage people in dialogue by asking questions taking polls, or requesting feedback. Make sure to share user-generated content, and provide credit to your followers or customers. Connect with influential people or industry experts by commenting on their content or by sharing their posts. Engage in relevant hashtags and participate in industry-specific discussions. Engaging with your customers and gaining their trust, you can improve your company's image, establish trust and build a strong audience for your company.

Section 4: Utilizing Paid Advertising

Social media platforms are effective advertising opportunities that increase your reach and bring visitors to your website or store online. Determine your goals for advertising that include creating brand awareness, producing leads or converting. Every platform has different types of ads, including Facebook advertisements, Instagram sponsored posts, as well as LinkedIn promoted content. Create a budget, determine your audience and make your ads engaging and unique which aligns with your company's brand. Examine your advertising's performance frequently and make changes to maximize the results. Paid advertisements can greatly boost the visibility of your social media as well as accelerate the growth of your small-scale business.

Section 5: Measuring Performance and Making Data-Driven Decisions

To make the most of your social media marketing efforts It is essential to evaluate results and make informed decisions. Utilize the tools for analytics offered by the various social media platforms to monitor metrics like engagement, reach web page clicks and conversions. Examine the data for insight into the preferences of your customers and the impact of your content and the performance of your marketing campaigns. Be able to make informed choices using this information, like altering the content strategy you employ, improving your target audience, or enhancing the effectiveness of your advertisements. Test and test again various strategies to improve your strategy for social media and enhance your results.

The conclusion is that in chapter 4, we examined the potential of social media, and how you can make use of to make your business more successful. If you select the appropriate platforms, creating an effective social media plan and engaging your customers through paid ads as well as making informed decisions to create an impressive online presence and increase awareness of your brand and help grow your business from home. Social media offers endless opportunities to reach out to your people, develop relationships and market your goods or products or. In the next section we'll dive into the world of online shopping and walk you through the steps to build an effective online store.

Chapter 25: Creating A Profitable E-Commerce Store

The internet offers a wealth of potential for entrepreneurs to connect with customers across the globe and make money by working from the comfort of their home. If you are aware of the essential factors of a successful online store, and applying efficient strategies, you will make sure you are on the right track to long-term success.

Section 1: Choosing Your E-commerce Platform

The initial step to making an online shop is to select the best platform to meet your needs. The most popular options are Shopify, WooCommerce, and BigCommerce. Take into consideration factors like user-friendliness, the number of available capabilities, customisation options as well as scalability and price. Choose platforms with intuitive interfaces for users as well as robust inventory management secured payment gateways that are secure with responsive themes and SEO features. Use free trial or demos to try various platforms prior to making an informed choice. When you've decided on one platform, you must adhere to the step-bystep set-up guides that are provided for registering your domain, set up shipping options, establish payment gateways and then customize your website's design.

Section 2: Selecting and Sourcing Products

Selection of the right products is a crucial aspect of the performance of your online store. Do extensive market research to find profitable niches and items that meet the needs of your customers and desires. Think about factors like the competition, demand for market profits margins, as well as the possibility of growth. Decide if you'll source items from wholesalers Dropshipping or dropshipping companies or make your own items. Find suppliers that offer top-quality goods, affordable prices as well as reliable delivery as well as excellent service to customers. Try out products prior to committing to large orders in order to guarantee their high-quality and appeal.Explore possibilities for customizing your own private label or packages of products that differentiate you from your competition.

Section 3: Designing a User-Friendly Website

A visually appealing and easy-to-use site is crucial for keeping and attracting clients. Choose an attractive theme, or work with a skilled web designer to develop your own design, which reflects your company's brand image. Design your website to be optimized for mobile devices so that you can provide a smooth user experience across different screen dimensions. Your products should be organized into pertinent areas and utilize clearly-defined navigation menus to allow users to locate the information they're seeking. Utilize advanced search capabilities as well as filtering features to boost the experience for users. Make sure to create compelling page designs with top-quality images along with detailed descriptions, user testimonials, and clear call-to-actions. Create a simple checkout procedure that offers a variety of secure payment options for building trust and reducing cart abandonment.

Section 4: Implementing Effective Marketing Strategies

Marketing is essential in driving traffic to your site and creating sales for your online store. Create a complete marketing strategy that includes organic as well as paid methods. Begin by optimizing your listings for products with appropriate words, compelling descriptions and meta tags for better the visibility of your search engines. Make use of social media to promote your product and engage your customers and conduct targeted advertising campaigns. Create content marketing using blogs, videos, or infographics which provide the value you want to give your public and showcase your skills. Set up an email database and use email marketing strategies to build connections with your clients and encourage customers to return purchases. Work with influencers, or create an affiliate program to broaden the reach of your business and engage new customers. Review your efforts regularly and track the key metrics and then refine your strategies using the information in order to get the most value from your investments.

Section 5: Providing Exceptional Customer Service

Excellent customer service is an essential aspect to operating a successful online store. It is essential to respond quickly to customer queries, be it via live chat, email or via phone. Create a simple returns and refunds policy in order to increase confidence and trust of your company's image. Customize your customer's experience with personalized emails and offering special discounts or creating a loyalty programme. Let customers leave feedback and reviews in order to generate social proof, and also attract new customers. Utilize feedback from customers to continually optimize your offerings, services and overall shopping experience. Connect with your customers through social media Respond to feedback and messages and resolve all concerns and questions quickly. Through providing excellent service to customers, you'll create a strong customers and earn positive word-of-mouth recommendations.

Section 6: Optimizing Conversion Rates and Retention Strategies

Making sure that conversion rates are optimized and using successful retention strategies are essential to the success long-term for your e-commerce business. In this part we'll look at strategies to increase conversion rates for customers and to encourage customers to make repeat purchases.

Streamline the Checkout Procedure 1. Simplify checkout in order to decrease friction and boost the number of conversions. Create a guest checkout method to ease the process for visitors who are new to the store. Make it easier to manage the entire process, reduce form fields and give customers a range of safe payment options. Show trust symbolism for example, SSL certificates or security badges to assure consumers about the security of their information.

Implement abandoned cart Recovery: A lot of customers leave their carts prior to making a purchase. Create an automated process for recovery of abandoned carts to contact customers to encourage customers to finish their purchases. Make personalized reminders via email with clear calls-to-action, and offer a reward for them, like a special discount or free shipping, in order to draw them to come back.

Present personalized product recommendations: Use information analytics as well as customer behaviour to provide specific product suggestions. Show related products or similar ones on the product's pages, or subsequent emails. Through suggesting products that are relevant will increase the your average order value, and even cross-sell your customers to the right products, thus improving sales and customer satisfaction.

Increase Customer Trust through Reviews and Testimonials: Display testimonials, reviews and testimonials in prominent places on your site. Positive reviews serve as social proof and impact buying decisions. Inviting satisfied customers to write reviews and display the reviews on product websites. React to feedback whether they are positive or negative and show your commitment to the satisfaction of your customers.

Create the Customer Loyalty Program Develop a loyalty program for customers to encourage repeat purchases as well as encourage loyalty from customers. Provide exclusive discounts, earlier access to sales or other perks for customers who are members of the loyalty program. Through nurturing relationships with customers by offering rewards that encourage your customers to buy from you again and become customers who are brand ambassadors.

Provide Outstanding Customer Support Post-purchase: A customer's experience doesn't stop after making the purchase. Offer excellent support post purchase to improve customer satisfaction and increase loyalty. Email order confirmations with details about tracking. Contact customers following the delivery date to make sure they are satisfied and to provide support if required. React quickly to questions or concerns, offering prompt solutions to increase trust and preserve an image of a good brand.

Use Retargeting Campaigns to Increase Sales Retargeting campaigns can be used for customers who already visited your site but not made an purchase. Display them ads that are personalized and based on the items they browsed through in order to entice them back to complete the purchase. Make use of compelling copywriting and images to engage the potential buyers and bring them back to the value your product can provide.

Through optimizing conversion rates by implementing efficient retention strategies, you'll be able to enhance the value every customer's retention, and generate the long-term success of your online business.

Chapter 26: Generating Passive Income Through Affiliate Marketing

Affiliate marketing can provide you with the opportunity to earn a commission by advertising other companies' products or services. When you understand the basic principles of affiliate marketing and using efficient strategies, you will be able to earn a steady income which can supplement your home-based business.

Section 1: Understanding Affiliate Marketing

To be successful in the realm in affiliate marketing it's vital to be able to demonstrate a clear grasp of its fundamental principles. The concept of affiliate marketing is performance-based model wherein you are paid an income from promoting and driving sales, or other specific actions that you want to do for other businesses and their products or products or. As an affiliate marketing professional, you serve as a link between your company and the end-user, making use of your website's platform and marketing efforts to earn income.

One of the major benefits that affiliate marketing has is the lower hurdle for access. It is not necessary to develop the products or services you want to sell and invest in inventory or provide customer support. Instead, concentrate on marketing products already popular and have been proven to be successful in converting. This lets you access markets that are already in place and make use of established brands.

In order to begin your journey into affiliate marketing, it is necessary to identify reputable affiliate program or networks that match the niche you are in and your target market. Affiliate networks like Amazon Associates, ShareASale, and ClickBank provide many options of services and products to select from. These companies are intermediaries that connect the companies seeking affiliates who can promote their products. Choose affiliate programs and research them to ensure they provide competitive commission rates, provide accurate tracking and reports as well as help and assistance for affiliates.

After you've selected the affiliate plan, you'll get a unique affiliate hyperlink or ID, which will track the revenue and traffic generated by your marketing actions. It is important to declare your affiliation with an open and honest manner in order so that you can maintain trust with the people who visit your site. This can be done by putting a disclaimer in the website, or inside your blog posts.

Section 2: Finding the Right Affiliate Programs

For success in affiliate marketing, it's essential to choose the best affiliate programs that are in line to your target customers. Begin by looking into reputable affiliate networks like Amazon Associates, ShareASale, or ClickBank that allow affiliates to connect with a diverse array of goods and services. Look through affiliate directories, or look for companies or products that are in your area of expertise. Take into consideration factors like commission rates, the duration of cookie products' quality and the reliability for the company's affiliate programs. Find affiliate companies which provide complete affiliate materials like banners, images of products as well as promotional material.

Section 3: Building an Engaging Affiliate Marketing Strategy

In order to maximize the earnings you earn as an affiliate marketer it's crucial to develop an effective and well-rounded affiliate marketing strategies. Get to know your customers' requirements, preferences, as well as problems. Determine the items or services they would like and provide worth. Develop informational content that informs, educates and promotes the products in a natural way. Integrate affiliate links seamlessly into your articles, while ensuring the transparency of your affiliation with affiliates to keep the trust of your readers.

Make use of a mixture of formats like blogs video reviews, product reviews or posts on social media in order to market affiliate products in a way that is effective. Provide personal stories, testimonials or case studies in order to establish credibility and demonstrate the way in which your product or service will help your customers. Offer genuine suggestions from your personal experience or deep investigation.

Make your site or platform more efficient for affiliate marketing by establishing special landing pages for affiliate marketing or guidebooks for comparison. The pages could showcase a range of affiliate offerings, and provide information about the benefits and features of each and distinctive selling points. Make persuasive calls to action that inspire people to click the affiliate link and then decide to purchase.

Include email marketing in your plan to build your customers and to encourage affiliate products. Make an email list, and develop valuable information that addresses your customers' issues or suggests solutions. Sort your list of email subscribers by interests or preference to provide specific advice. Offer exclusive deals or special promotions to motivate your readers to buy something through your affiliate link.

Section 4: Tracking and Analyzing Affiliate Performance

Monitoring and analysing the results in your affiliate marketing campaigns is essential to optimize your plan and maximising the amount of money you make. Utilize affiliate tracking tools and integrated reporting tools offered by affiliate networks to track the number of clicks, conversions and commissions. Find out which affiliate products and promotions yield the most result. Review key indicators, including click-through rates or conversion rates as well as the earnings per click, to assess the efficacy of your promotions.

Try different affiliate programs as well as products and promotional techniques to discover the most effective combination. Test different strategies like various formats of content or the placement of affiliate links, in order to find the tactics that are most popular and resonate most with your target audience. Continue to improve your affiliate marketing plan by analyzing the data and knowledge you gain.

Section 5: Building Long-Term Relationships

Establishing lasting and strong relations to your associate partners are essential for success over the long term within the field of affiliate marketing. If you nurture these relationships, you will be able to unlock more opportunities, and gain access to special benefits that will increase the potential of your earnings.

The first and most important thing is that open and honest communications are essential. Engage regularly with your partners from affiliates, giving feedback on the product's performances, sharing suggestions to collaborate, or discussing possible promotional possibilities. This creates a feeling of collaboration and demonstrates your commitment to mutual success.

Partner with affiliates to develop exclusive deals or special discounts that you can distributed to your followers. It not only provides the value of your customers however it can also increase conversion and generate more sales through your affiliate link. With unique incentive programs it allows you to differentiate your affiliate from others and maximize your potential earnings.

When you are established as a reputable affiliate you could gain access to superior product details and pre-launch offers, as well as exclusive offers. The majority of affiliate partners appreciate affiliates that consistently boost sales and market their goods successfully. This may result in increased percentages of commission, greater visibility and many other advantages which can dramatically impact the amount you earn.

Always monitor the progress of the affiliate program you're promoting. Review key performance indicators like the conversion rate, earning per click, or price to find the most lucrative partnerships. Concentrate your efforts on strategies that yield the highest results, and then think about making adjustments or stopping programs which aren't performing.. Always review and adjust your approach based on results and information you've gathered.

Establishing long-lasting relationships with your associate partners isn't just about financial gains, but is in addition, it is about mutual support and expansion. You can share the stories of your success, provide testimonials, and make sure to promote your affiliate partners to your local or regional network. It demonstrates your enthusiasm about their products, and can help to strengthen the relationship that you have with your associate partners.

Through establishing strong relationships between your partners you'll be able to create an affiliate marketing venture that earns an ongoing stream of income as well as opens the door for exciting possibilities to come up with exciting opportunities in the future.

Final Conclusion The conclusion is that in Chapter 6, we looked at the notion of earning passive income using affiliate marketing. If you are able to understand the basics of affiliate marketing and identifying the most appropriate affiliate marketing programs, creating an effective affiliate marketing plan monitoring and analysing outcomes, and establishing ongoing relationships with associate partners, you will be able to earn a steady income that can supplement your home-based enterprise. Affiliate marketing can provide you with the possibility to earn a commission by promoting goods or services that match with the needs of your target audience. In the next section we'll explore the realm of freelance work and remote work, examining ways to learn the art of freelance writing for a living.

Chapter 27: Mastering The Art Of Freelancing And Remote Services

The freedom of freelance allows you to provide your talents and knowledge to clients across the globe by offering services from the comfort of your home. If you are aware of the fundamentals of freelance work and applying efficient strategies, you will be able to develop a lucrative freelance enterprise and experience the freedom and flexibility that come with the freedom of being a freelancer.

Section 1: Identifying Your Freelance Skills

When you begin your journey as a freelancer It is crucial to determine and develop the specific abilities you have. Examine your skills in your field, interests, and expertise to identify the kind of capabilities you are able to offer customers who might be interested. Think about your work experience and education level, as well as certifications and any specific knowledge you've got.

Consider your talents and passions Consider how these are in line with the requirements of market. Are you a skilled graphic designer, writer marketer, developer of websites, translator or consultant? Find out what skills you are able to make use of to provide the best value to your clients and satisfy their needs.

Conduct market research in order to determine what skills are needed. Look into freelancing sites such as job boards, job sites, as well as industry trends, to determine the needs of the market and possible chances. Consider areas where your talents are highly sought-after and where the competition is low. This will help you create your own niche and establish yourself as the expert in a particular area or sector.

Take note of the ever-changing requirements of the market as well as the latest trends. Be aware of the latest developments in your industry and update your knowledge to meet the needs of your industry. Learn and improve your knowledge through online classes as well as workshops and training programs for mentors. In keeping up-to-date and current your business can be attractive to clients looking for the most up-to-date information and skills.

Section 2: Building a Strong Online Presence

A strong online presence is essential to building your reputation as a reliable freelancer, and also attracting new customers. A properly designed online presence shows the expertise, knowledge as well as professionalism. These are the ways to create a powerful online presence

Create a professional site Create a professional site which serves as your online portfolio, and displays your work. Include an easy-to-read biography, information about your offerings, examples of your work and positive testimonials from your clients. Your website should be attractive, simple to use, and optimised to be indexed by Google and other search engines.

Make use of Social Media: Use social media sites like LinkedIn, Twitter, Instagram and Facebook to advertise your services as a freelancer. Select platforms that are in alignment with the target market and your industries. Engage with your followers, as well as participate in discussions about industry issues. Make yourself known as an expert with your insights, advice and useful information that will make your brand more attractive to potential customers.

Network Online: Join forums, online communities and freelance platforms to meet other freelancers as well as potential customers. Join discussions, provide suggestions, and offer your experience. Find out about freelance work opportunities, and take part in webinars or industry events to build your network.

Highlight Your Work: Develop a strong portfolio of your finest works. Be sure to include several projects that demonstrate your flexibility as well as your expertise. If you're just beginning out and aren't working in a professional capacity take on the pro bono or personal tasks to increase your resume.

Collect Testimonials: Request reviews from happy customers and post the testimonials on your site or your portfolio. Testimonials provide credibility and social proof. They can dramatically increase the credibility of your business and increase trustworthiness.

Be Consistent: Keep an image of your brand that is consistent across all of your social media platforms. Make sure you use professional profile photos with consistent branding as well as a consistent message that represents your knowledge and beliefs. A consistent approach builds trust and credibility with potential customers.

When you establish a robust web presence, you boost your exposure and allow clients to connect to them. This establishes you as a reliable and dependable freelancer and sets the tone for success in client engagements as well as lasting business relationships.

Section 3: Setting Freelance Rates and Negotiating Contracts

The process of determining your rates for freelance work isn't easy, but it's essential to ensure a steady earnings. Find out the industry standard, think about the level of your knowledge and your value to your clients. Determine your fees according to the difficulty of the task as well as the time commitment required and the level of quality you provide.

Increase your rate gradually as you get greater experience and create an impressive portfolio.

In negotiating contracts with your clients, make clear the project goals, deadlines, deliverables and the payment conditions. You can protect your interests signing written contracts or service agreements which outline the specifics for the undertaking. You should be transparent regarding your availability as well as your preferences for communication and your revision policy to avoid confusion later.

Section 4: Managing Client Relationships and Delivering Exceptional Service

The development of strong client relationships is vital to the long-term viability of freelancer. Engage quickly, professionally effectively and professionally with your customers and ensure that you are aware of the expectations and needs of your clients. Keep clients informed of the progress of your project, solicit comments, and resolve any questions or concerns they might be asking.

Provide exceptional customer service by continuously keeping deadlines in mind, delivering top-quality services, doing your best in order to surpass the client's expectations. Set out to earn a name in professionalism, reliability and outstanding customer service. Build long-lasting relationships by building relationships, providing ongoing assistance, and delivering additional value over the course of the initiative.

Section 5: Continuously Upgrading Skills and Expanding Services

In order to succeed as a freelancer is to have an attitude of continual development and learning. The landscape of freelance is constantly evolving in the face of new technologies and market trends that are changing and new demands from clients. If you keep on improving your abilities and expanding your capabilities, you'll be able to remain ahead of the game and remain competitive within the field.

Keep Up-to-date with Industry trends: Stay informed on the newest trends in your industry in innovation, best practices, and techniques.

Follow industry thought-leaders, magazines, as well as relevant blogs to keep up-to-date on new developments within your field. Participate in professional groups, take part in webcasts, or attend trade shows to learn more and connect with colleagues. The continuous learning process lets you know the ever-changing demands of customers and adjust your abilities and service offerings to meet them.

Make sure you invest in your professional development Plan your time and funds to professional development to improve your abilities and increase your understanding. Make use of online courses such as workshops, certifications, or seminars which focus on topics pertinent to your freelance job. If you invest in yourself you show your dedication to provide exceptional customer service as well as being up to date with advancements in the field.

Diversify Your Skills You should consider the possibility of expanding your knowledge so that you can meet a greater spectrum of needs for clients. Find complementary services or skills which complement your current skills. As an example, if you're a web developer and you want to learn the front end development as well as UX/UI design so that you can give a fuller service for clients. The ability to diversify your skills does more than increase your potential for marketability, but will also provide possibilities for new income streams.

Provide Specialized Services Although diversification is beneficial but there's also benefit to focusing on an area of expertise. Find niches in your field with high demand and little competition. If you are an expert in one certain area, you can position yourself as an authority and will attract customers who are looking for specific skills. This lets you charge more rates as well as establish yourself as a professional who delivers outstanding results in your field of expertise.

Get Feedback and learn From Experience: Actively get feedback from clients, and gain knowledge from each assignment or task. Consider your strengths as well as areas for enhancement. Find patterns in feedback from clients and make use of this as a guideline for development. Utilize constructive criticism as an opportunity to improve the skills you have and increase your offerings. Be determined to always exceed your client's expectations and produce outstanding results.

Collaborate with other freelancers Working with freelancers from other companies can be beneficial for both parties and assist you in expanding the scope of your services. Collaborate with freelancers with the same skills or experience in order to provide complete solutions for clients. A collaborative strategy lets you access a an array of opportunities and meet clients' varied requirements.

Be Flexible: Take advantage of the change in your environment and remain open to the possibility of new opportunities. The landscape of freelance work is constantly changing as new developments or new trends could change the way you work. Be flexible and ready to acquire new tools and technologies, or adapt your offerings in order to satisfy changing needs of your clients. Becoming a part of the change process and remaining in the forefront will make you an innovative freelancer that can take advantage of the constantly changing landscape.

In constant improvement of your expertise and diversifying your offerings by seeking feedback and remaining flexible and flexible, you will make sure your career as a freelancer continues to be relevant and profitable. Take advantage of lifelong learning and an attitude of continuous advancement to take advantage of new opportunities and to sustain your long-term growth.

Final Conclusion 7th Chapter: In Chapter 7 we looked into the realm of remote and freelancing. Through identifying the skills you have for freelance and establishing a solid online presence, setting attractive rates, establishing client relations and constantly enhancing your abilities, you will be able to learn the art of freelance and build a profitable career that is fulfilling working from the comfort at home. It is a way to earn a living, versatility, and the potential to earn an income of a significant amount. In the next section we'll look at the possibility of launching an online training course, or coaching businesses.

Chapter 28: Launching A Successful Online Course Or Coaching Business

The need for online education as well as personal development has exploded over the last few years, creating the opportunity to earn money for those with expertise and knowledge to impart. Utilizing your expertise and talents, you could make and sell educational materials and empower others, while creating an income-generating home business.

Section 1: Defining Your Course or Coaching Offer

When you are launching an online course or a coaching company it is important to identify your product and determine the audience that you would like to target. Begin by reviewing your experience of skills, abilities, and experience. What insights are you able to provide? What issues or obstacles will you be able to help your readers over?

Find a subject that is suited to your needs and make sure it is in line with the needs and interests of the target group. Do market research to confirm the market demand for your selected topic. Find existing courses or instructors in similar fields and study their offers prices, as well as customer feedback. Find out what unique value you offer and the ways you will stand out from your competitors.

Be aware of your intended audience's preferences and preferred learning styles. Is your course either video-based or text-based? Or the combination of all three? Choose the best format that fits your material and connects with your target audience. Also, determine what level of support that you'll provide in the form of one-on-one coaching, group coaching or an online learning course.

Section 2: Creating Compelling Course Content or Coaching Framework

In order to launch an online coaching course or business, you need to produce engaging and relevant material that is engaging for your viewers. The first step is to outline the primary topics or sessions for coaching to be discussed. Then break the information into manageable sections, and make sure you have that the subjects are logically arranged.

Make course-related materials like instructional videos, slide slides and workbooks. You can also create quizzes or downloads that match the teaching method you employ. Create your material to be engaging, informative and practical, offering concrete exercises and illustrations that enhance learning.

Use multimedia components including images, graphics or animations, in order to make your lesson interesting and visually appealing. Use storytelling methods to engage your learners and bring ideas to reality. Think about including case studies from real life and testimonials or even success stories that inspire and encourage your students.

If you provide coaching, you must create the framework which outlines the coaching process. Determine the outcomes and objectives the clients are expected to be able to achieve with your coaching programs. Create templates or tools that help facilitate your coaching journey as well as provide the structure of your sessions.

Section 3: Building Your Online Course Platform or Coaching Brand

When you've established your content for your course or created a coach's framework and have established your framework for coaching, it's time to establish your online presence and build your own brand. Develop a unique web page or landing page that highlights the course you offer or your coaching services. Make use of compelling text and images to highlight the advantages and value to customers or potential students.

Pick an online course platform or a coaching management system which meets your requirements. Take into consideration factors like the ease of use, scaling as well as payment processing features as well as marketing capabilities. The most popular online courses include Teachable, Thinkific, or Kajabi as well as coaches management software alternatives are platforms such as CoachAccountable as well as Acuity Scheduling.

Develop effective marketing strategies that reach your intended public. Utilize the social media channels such as emails, content marketing as well as paid ads for promoting your course or coaching service. Give away free materials including e-books mini-courses or webinars to grow your list of email subscribers and build relationships with prospective students or customers.

Build your reputation and credibility through the creation of valuable material on your blog, by guest blogging on related websites or being an interviewer on podcasts or webinars. Engage your followers on social media, address queries, and provide useful information to increase credibility and make yourself known as an authority within your area.

Section 4: Marketing and Promoting Your Course or Coaching Services

Promotion and marketing have a major impact on the growth of an online course or coaching company. In order to increase the reach of your business and to attract new customers or learners, you must implement successful marketing strategies that cater to the target market. Below are a few key actions to take into consideration:

Create a Marketing Strategy and outline your objectives for marketing and objectives, your target audience, the messaging and channels that will reach your desired clients or learners. Determine the social media platforms on which your intended audience is the most active, and then tailor your marketing strategy to meet their needs.

Design Compelling sales Copy Write compelling and informative sales materials that clearly presents the benefits and worth of your program or coaching service. Then, highlight the way your offer addresses a particular issue or fulfills a critical requirement for your intended audience.

Use Content Marketing to Make valuable content like blog posts, videos or podcasts which provide information, advice or useful info relevant to your training or niche of coaching. Make sure to share this information on your site and social media channels, along with other appropriate channels to engage and attract your audience.

Use email marketing to your advantage Make an email database with a lead-generating offer like a free ebook and checklists, or a small-sized courses related to your course or topic for coaching. Keep your list members engaged with relevant material and promotions to make them pay-per-click clients.

Collaboration with influencers or Affiliates: Collaborate with affiliates or influencers within your field who have a good online presence and appropriate target audience. Create content together, give them promotional discounts or provide these individuals with affiliate links to advertise your courses or coaching service.

Don't forget to offer limited-time offers Create an impression of urgency and exclusivity through giving limited-time discounts or discounts for early bird customers to encourage potential students or customers to sign up or reserve your coaching services.

Section 5: Providing Exceptional Learning or Coaching Experiences

A memorable training or learning experience is the key to building customers' trust and encouraging positive recommendations. Here are a few strategies you can employ to provide exceptional experiences for the clients and learners you serve:

Create a supportive learning Environment: Create a positive and stimulating learning environment for the students in your class. Facilitate collaboration and interaction through discussions forums, live Q&A discussions as well as group coaching calls. Inspire learners to communicate their thoughts and experience and build a sense of the community.

Customize your Coaching Sessions: Customize your coaching sessions to suit the individual needs and goals of every client. Design a customized action plan, provide targeted feedback, as well as provide continuous assistance to assist clients in achieving the goals they desire.

Continuous communication: Keep an open and regular communications with your students or customers. Offer prompt answers to their questions or issues as well as provide additional information or assistance when required. Check regularly on the progress of their work and provide encouragement and accountability.

Ask for Feedback and adjust Get feedback from your students or clients in order to improve the content of your courses or coaching strategies. Take surveys, gather testimonials and listen attentively to their feedback. Continue to improve your products and services in response to the comments received.

Give Post-Course and Post-Coaching Assistance: Offer coaching or post-course support to make sure your students or clients are able to apply their new abilities or knowledge efficiently. Give them additional resources, regular access to course materials and follow-up coaching sessions in order to help them continue their development and achievement.

Final Conclusion The conclusion is that in Chapter 8 we looked at the method of the launch of a successful online coaching course or business. Through defining your course, or offer of coaching, developing captivating content or an effective the framework for coaching, creating your brand and online presence as well as implementing effective marketing tactics, you are able to make yourself an authority within your field, and create revenue while having a positive impression on your students or customers. If you provide exceptional training or learning experiences that build customer loyalty and trigger a chain reaction of referrals that are positive. In the next section we'll explore the realm of dropshipping and fulfillment solutions, examining the ways you can use this method to build an online business that is scalable.

Chapter 29: Exploring The World Of Dropshipping And Fulfillment Services

Dropshipping takes away the requirement to manage inventory and fulfill orders so you can concentrate on customer service and marketing. If you are aware of the fundamentals of dropshipping, and applying efficient strategies, you will be able to develop a profitable online shop without a significant upfront expenditure.

Section 1: Understanding the Dropshipping Model

In order to succeed with dropshipping, you must understand the basics of this method. When you dropship, you function as a middleman between buyer and supplier. Instead of stocking and directing your inventory, you buy goods from suppliers outside of your own who take care of inventory storage as well as shipping.

Find trusted suppliers that offer high-end items and effective fulfillment methods. Dropshipping platforms like AliExpress, Oberlo, or SaleHoo will connect you to many vendors and items.

Examine suppliers thoroughly, focusing on things like the quality of their products delivery times, product quality, as well as the reviews of customers.

Develop a smooth process to fulfill orders by connecting your website with supplier's systems. When a client makes an order through your website, it's transferred to the supplier, which then takes care of packing and shipping directly to the buyer. This streamline approach lets your focus to be on customer service, marketing as well as growing your business.

Section 2: Selecting a Profitable Niche and Products

Picking a profitable market is vital to the success of your dropshipping business. Conduct market research in order to find the trends, demand as well as niches that are not being served. Choose products with enough market share and the right balance between demands and competitors.

Take into consideration factors like product distinctiveness, profitability margins and the target audience's appeal when choosing the products you choose. Find products that are in alignment with your passions or interests to ensure that you remain in the loop and educated about the products you offer.

Test your product concepts by using the internet and social media platforms, as well as the feedback of customers. Review search volume competitors, search volume, as well as customer feedback to determine the viability of the market. Ask for feedback from clients or experts in the industry to assess interest and gain data.

When you've selected your field select a set of items that meet the needs of your audience and preference. Try to find a mixture of the top selling products, trendy products, as well as niche-specific items that cater to a broad spectrum of consumer interests.

Section 3: Setting Up Your Online Store

A professional, user-friendly online store is vital to creating credibility and drawing in clients.

The following steps will help you establish your dropshipping business:

Select an online store which is suitable for your requirements for your business, like Shopify, WooCommerce, or BigCommerce. These platforms provide an intuitive user interface, theme customization and dropshipping integrations applications.

Pick a pleasing and visually appealing design that is consistent with your branding and products. Modify the theme to make an unforgettable and unique online store.

Make your pages more efficient with compelling descriptions of your products with high-quality photos or videos. Also, you can display the reviews of customers or their ratings. Facilitate the purchase process and secure by using secure payment processors.

Use efficient search engine optimization (SEO) strategies that will increase your shop's ranking on search results. Find relevant keywords, improve the titles and descriptions of your products and create quality backlinks that will boost your store's online visibility.

Automated mail marketing campaigns that engage customers, announce new products and to encourage returning purchase. Give incentives like discount coupons or special content to increase customer loyalty.

Section 4: Marketing and Promoting Your Dropshipping Store

A well-planned marketing strategy is essential to increasing traffic and sales to your dropshipping shop. Use a combination of marketing techniques online to draw in new customers and create brand awareness.

Utilize social media platforms including TikTok, Facebook, Instagram as well as Pinterest to show off your offerings, interact with your audience and create targeted ads. Design visually pleasing material, work with influential people as well as use analytics on social media to improve your marketing campaigns.

Put money into the search engine marketing (SEM) through the use of Google Ads or Bing

Ads to reach customers who are actively looking for items that are related to your industry. Do keyword research, design appealing ad content, and improve your campaign so that you can maximize the conversion rates.

Content marketing is also an effective strategy. Make informative video posts, blog entries or guidebooks related to your field of expertise. Provide tips, information or instructional videos that connect with the people you want to reach. Make sure to share this content via your site and social media channels, and other relevant online communities to increase traffic to your site and establish the credibility of your business.

Make an email database with lead magnets, including free ebooks and checklists or even discounts. Make use of emails to build relationships with the leads, provide product recommendations, and advertise special deals as well as flash sales.

Use CRO or conversion rate optimization (CRO) methods to improve customer satisfaction and boost the efficiency of your shop's conversion rates. Make your pages more user-friendly optimize the checkout process and provide personalized suggestions according to the customer's preferences.

Section 5: Customer Service and Building Trust

A high-quality customer experience is vital to establish confidence and encouraging loyalty to your business. Make sure you provide the best experience and seamless for your clients.

Set up clear channels for communication and promptly respond to customer queries, questions or concerns. Provide multiple channels including email, chat on the go or social media channels for different customer needs.

You can guarantee efficient fulfillment of orders and expedited delivery by continuously communication with your suppliers. Keep track of order status, provide tracking information to your customers and deal with any issues or delays promptly.

Think about offering a guarantee of satisfaction or return policy that is hassle-free in order to create confidence with your clients. Resolve customer complaints or concerns quickly in a timely manner and provide solutions that go beyond the expectations of your customers.

Inviting customers to leave reviews or write testimonials, by providing incentives or a follow-up email when they have purchased. Reviews and testimonials that are positive provide social proof, and could significantly affect the reputation and credibility of your business.

Conclusion in Chapter 9 we talked about the subject of fulfillment and dropshipping. If you understand the model of dropshipping and identifying a lucrative niche and offering, setting up an online store, applying successful marketing strategies, as well as offering excellent customer support, you could create a profitable dropshipping company in the comfort at home.